BY THE EDITORS OF CONSUMER GUIDE®

PERENNIALS

Contributing Authors:
Carol Landa Christensen
Peter Loewer

Consultant:
Darrel Apps

Illustrator:
Mike Muir

BEEKMAN HOUSE

Photo Credits:

Contributors:

Carol Landa Christensen (chapters 1-5) graduated cum laude from the Pennsylvania School of Horticulture for Women, and went on to work at Longwood Gardens as a Horticulture Information Specialist and as a floral decorator. For the past seven years, she has been a feature writer for the Springfield (Massachusetts) newspapers, and was a frequent contributor to *Gurney's Gardening News* until it ceased publication.

Peter Loewer (encyclopedia) is the editor of the *Newsletter for the Garden Writers of America* and has written a number of books on gardening, including *Growing and Decorating with Grasses, American Gardens, The Annual Garden, Gardens by Design,* and *A Year of Flowers.* He is also a botanical illustrator. Mr. Loewer lives in Cochecton Center, New York, a small town in the Catskill Mountains.

Dr. Darrel Apps (consultant) was the departmental Head of Education at Longwood Gardens for 12 years before he began his own consulting and training business, Garden Adventures, at Chadds Ford, Pennsylvania. He is a frequent lecturer on horticultural topics and teaches courses on perennials. Dr. Apps is also a nationally recognized daylily hybridizer.

CONTENTS

CHAPTER 1   HOW TO PLAN FOR LASTING COLOR   4
             How's the Soil & Light ?   6
             Color   8
             Form & Texture   10
             Selecting Perennials for Color & Characteristics   14
             Sequence of Bloom   18
             Selecting Perennials by Bloom Date   20

CHAPTER 2   GETTING YOUR GARDEN OFF TO A GOOD START   22
             Tools for Gardening Projects   24
             Groundwork: Turning & Enriching the Earth   26
             Transplanting from Pots   29
             Setting Bare-Root Plants   32
             Buying Healthy Plants   34

CHAPTER 3   GIVE YOUR PERENNIALS LOTS OF CARE   36
             Watering, Weeding, & Feeding   38
             Ways to Increase/Control Growth   43
             Staking Garden Plants   46
             Pests & Other Problems   49
             Preparing for Winter   53
             Zone Map: The Last Frost in Your Area   56
             Maintaining Perennials Month by Month   58

CHAPTER 4   THE MAGIC OF PROPAGATING NEW PLANTS   60
             Starting from Seed   62
             Starting Stem & Root Cuttings   67
             Dividing Perennials   73

CHAPTER 5   LANDSCAPING WITH PERENNIALS   76
             Putting a Garden on Paper   78
             Entrance Gardens, Borders, & Island Beds   82
             Perennials in Containers   86
             Perennials for Wet Situations   88
             Rock Gardens   90

CHAPTER 6   ENCYCLOPEDIA OF PERENNIAL FAVORITES   92
             INDEX   141

This perennials border, tucked
in against a white picket fence,
illustrates the beauty of flowers
and foliage. The contrast of
ground-hugging foliage,
arching leaves and blooms,
and spiky foxgloves is indeed
a sight to behold.

CHAPTER 1

HOW TO PLAN FOR LASTING COLOR

Perennials are plants that survive winter outdoors to produce new growth and flowers each summer. Unlike annuals that flower continuously for several months, most perennials only bloom for two to three weeks. Therefore, it's necessary to plan your garden carefully, in order to have color in perennial beds during selected periods. By carefully working out a plan in advance on paper, you can be assured of a colorful show all season long.

It would be a mistake to place emphasis exclusively on perennial flowers. There is much beauty in the textures and subtle colors of perennial *foliage* as well. Spreading silver-gray mats of cerastium; bold hosta clumps in various shades of blue-green, green and white, and gold; the fine-laced fern fronds—the list of attractive foliage goes on and on. Those who grow perennials tend to be as aware of, and enthusiastic about, foliage as they are about flowers!

Whether you use just a few perennials in bold masses among shrubs or under trees, mix them in with annuals, or specialize in the many varieties of one particular kind, you'll find that perennials provide dependable beauty year after year.

How's the Soil & Light?

Hostas flourish in both sunlight and shade.

Soil and light are especially important factors when planning perennial planting. Along with water, they are the essential elements needed for successful gardening. We first need to know what kind of soil we have and to make any necessary adjustments, so it would be the best it can possibly be for growing plants. In the case of light, we must determine the amount that's available. With this information, we can make our plant selections: shade-loving plants for low-light areas; sun lovers for bright, sunny locations.

Let's talk about soil first. Soil types vary from the extremes of constantly dry, nutrient-poor sand to 90 percent rocks held together with 10 percent soil to rich, heavy clay (which forms a sticky, shoe-grabbing mass when wet, then dries to brick hardness). Fortunately, most soil conditions fall somewhere between these extremes. Still, very few homeowners find they have that ideal "rich garden loam" to work with!

Therefore, the first order of business is to learn just what kind of soil you *do* have. The way to do this is to have your soil tested. In some states, the county Cooperative Extension office will do soil-nutrient tests; in others, it's necessary to use the services of a private testing lab.

To obtain a representative sample of the soil in your flower bed, take a tablespoonful from each end of the bed and another from somewhere in the middle. Dig 4 to 6 inches down before taking each sample. Mix all of the samples together thoroughly in a single container. Then hand carry or mail the mixture to those doing the testing.

You'll want a complete soil test. One part will be a pH test that reads for acidity and alkalinity. A pH test result between 6.0 and 7.0 is ideal and requires no adjustment. A result below 6.0 indicates the soil is too acid. Ground limestone should be added to correct this problem. If the reading is over 7.2, the soil is too alkaline. To solve this problem, add powdered sulfur or, for quicker results, iron sulfate.

In addition to pH, you'll receive information about the nutrients in your soil. If there is a deficiency in any of these nutrients, you'll need to add the missing elements as recommended in the report. A third result will tell you the percentage of organic materials your soil contains; this information will help you decide whether or not you need to supplement your soil with additional organic matter. (Details on fertilizing and improving garden soil can be found in Chapter 3 in the section "Watering, Weeding, & Feeding," page 38.)

Some homesites have so little soil or the soil is so poor that it cannot—or should not—be used at all. One solution in these situations is to build raised beds and fill them with high-quality soil brought in from elsewhere. Such beds should be at least 6 inches deep to allow good root penetration. This may seem a costly solution in the short-term, but the beds will last for years and prove themselves well worth your initial investment.

Another solution, especially in a small area, is to garden entirely in containers. An imaginative approach, such as installing a deck or patio over the useless ground and then decorating it with container-grown plants, can transform a sad eyesore into an oasis. (You'll find more details on container gardening in Chapter 5, page 86.)

Light is another important factor in gardening. How much is there and for how many hours each day? In other words, does the area where you want to grow perennials have full sun, partial shade, or full shade?

At least to some extent, the amount of light the flower bed receives will dictate the plant species you'll be able to grow. Those plants that love full sun may become leggy and produce very few flowers if they're planted in a shady spot. By the same token, some plants are sensitive to too much light and will burn when placed in bright sunlight. Fortunately, there are perennials suited to all kinds of light conditions. Therefore, except for those places of deepest shade, there are many different kinds from which to choose.

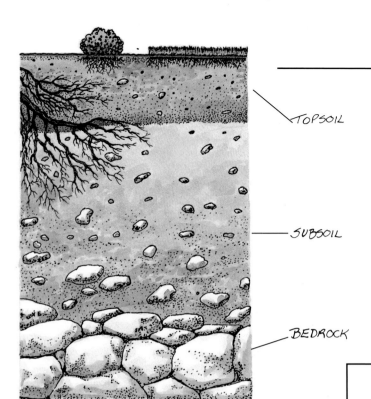

TOPSOIL

SUBSOIL

BEDROCK

Typical Soil Profile

A typical soil profile contains three basic layers: topsoil, subsoil, and bedrock. The depth of each of these layers varies tremendously. In New England alone, there are hilly areas where only 1 inch of topsoil and 1 inch of subsoil are found on top of the bedrock, while nearby valleys have 15 inches of topsoil before subsoil is reached. Where there is insufficient topsoil, it is necessary to supplement it—perhaps in raised beds or behind a retaining wall—before perennials can be grown. Dig a straight-sided hole to see your soil profile.

Testing for Soil Type

Soil may vary from light sand to heavy clay. A rough test can be made by squeezing a wettened sample in your hand. If it falls apart easily, it's primarily sand; if it forms a solid, sticky glob, it's primarily clay. The ideal growing medium is somewhere between the two; by adding conditioners and humus to your soil, you can make it closer to that ideal. Send a soil sample to a testing lab to learn what additives and nutrients your soil needs.

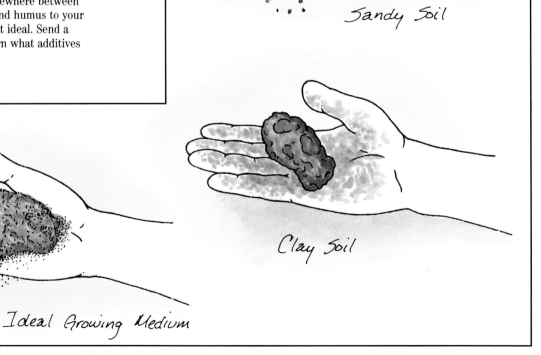

Sandy Soil

Clay Soil

Ideal Growing Medium

Color

There are several aspects of color that need to be considered when planning perennial plantings. The primary source of color is, of course, from flowers. But another equally important consideration is the color provided by existing backgrounds: fences, house walls, flowering shrubs, or the blossoms in neighboring gardens. If, for example, the background is painted white, white flowers planted against it will become virtually invisible. If the background contains bright red flowers, you may not want the vivid contrast that purple blooms would add. If the area is backed by dark woods or evergreens, you should keep in mind that dark shades of blue and purple will disappear; whites, yellows, silver-grays, and yellow-greens will stand out.

In addition to such physical considerations, there are also emotional ones: Color can be mood setting. Red, yellow, and orange shades are bright, warm, and cheering. On the other hand, blues, silvers, and whites are calming and cooling—they can be very soothing during the heat of summer. A nostalgic, romantic look can be achieved by using pale pastels; a modern, upbeat style results when pure bright colors are mixed. Think about the mood and atmosphere you'd like to create in each area of your garden; it may differ from one location to another and even from one season to the next.

If you feel uncertain about color, you may want to use proven combinations with the help of a color wheel. There are three basic winning combinations. The first is monochromatic—it combines all of the various shades, tints, and tones of a single color. The second is complementary, and includes all of the variations of two colors exactly opposite each other on the color wheel. The last is analogous—those variations of three colors that are found adjacent to one another on the color wheel. These are not the only possible combinations, but they are the easiest to use and the most certain to succeed.

Two final hints on color: 1) White flowers will blend easily with any other colors you select; and 2) Varying the intensity of different flower colors in your design will often help add vitality and interest to the planting.

Although you'll want to plan the colors for your garden with care, inevitably some of your choices will not work out as happily as you'd envisioned. Don't be *too* worried about getting it all exactly right in advance. You can always move or remove those plants that do not blend well. Part of the fun in gardening is to make adjustments and changes from season to season.

This planting of perennials has a nostalgic, romantic look.

Full Color Wheel

A color wheel can be a helpful tool in choosing flower colors that blend well together. All of the shades, tints, and tones, as well as the pure color of any spoke on the color wheel, will automatically combine well.

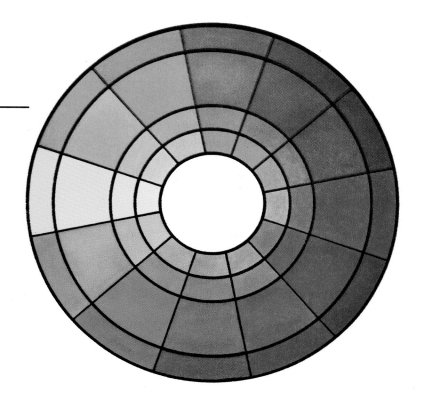

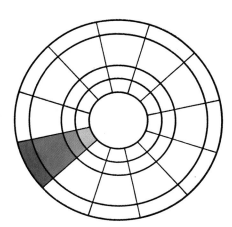

Monochromatic Colors

A monochromatic design is one in which all of the flower colors are in a single color line. The only variety will be in their range—from dark, to intense, to pastel shades of that one color: i.e., from navy blue, to bright blue, to baby blue.

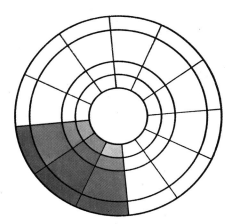

Analogous Colors

Analogous designs include flowers of any of the hues in any three spokes that are side-by-side on the color wheel: for example, all the blue shades, plus all of the blue-violet shades, and all of the violet shades.

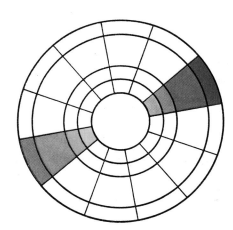

Complementary Colors

Using two colors opposite each other on the color wheel will produce a complementary color scheme. Starting again with blue, this would blend all of the clear blues with all of the clear oranges.

Form &
Texture

Contrast of color, form, and texture can be very pleasing.

Most people give little thought to the forms and textures of plants, even though they are important aspects of perennials because, for a good part of the growing season when they're not in bloom, that's all that is to be enjoyed. In fact, in the case of some perennials, form and texture are *all* that matters: fern clumps take us from the early spring unfolding of their fiddleheads through the fully open filigree of their fronds and on to their golden autumn color. Flowers are not used for this effect at all. Many hostas, stonecrops, and ornamental grasses are also better known for their foliage effects than for their flowers. In other cases, plants may have two very different forms, depending on whether or not they are in bloom. In these instances, it is better to use the forms of these plants when they are not in bloom.

An extra bonus to be savored and utilized in the landscape is a plant that has lovely blossoms as well as an attractive growth habit. The flowers themselves vary in form and texture, too: the huge, airy clouds of baby's breath; tall, handsome spires of delphinium and foxtail lilies; the round pompoms of chrysanthemums and peonies; and the graceful arches of bleeding heart—each bloom perfectly heart-shaped.

Among perennials, there are some outstandingly handsome examples of foliage and form. Peonies have a rugged, bold leaf cluster that turns to wonderful shades of pink or bronze in the autumn; hostas provide dramatic low clumps that can be used alone or combined with other plants; the blue-gray globe thistle foliage makes a handsome bush; and the tall, slender Japanese and Siberian iris foliage provides a wonderful spiky contrast to round-leaved neighbors.

Fortunately, many perennials offer this added bonus of interesting texture and/or form to the garden. In many instances, they also offer a color contrast as well. Use plants with these bonuses wherever possible, although it doesn't mean you should completely bypass those that only have attractive blooms to their credit. Instead, intermix the outstanding stars with the duller kinds. A good idea is to intermingle the various forms and textures of perennials or to repeat forms at regular intervals for a sense of rhythm and flow. In a smaller garden, finer, feathery textures should dominate; in a larger garden, there is sufficient space for coarse textures to be prevalent. Using these simple hints, you'll produce a completed planting, which is interesting throughout the growing season—whether in bloom or not.

The Varied Forms of Perennials

The form, or shape, of perennials is important to consider when designing a garden. By selecting plants with varying forms, the garden will be more interesting to look at. Ground-hugging mats; tall, spiked growth; as well as arching and rounded plants provide a visual variety you'll enjoy even when the plants aren't in bloom.

Ground-hugging

Arching

Tall & Spiked

Rounded

Textures of Perennials

A variety of textures adds to a garden's beauty. Placing plants with feathery foliage or flowers next to ones that have coarse, bold characteristics will produce a dramatic-looking garden. It's helpful to pretest how plants will look together by placing potted samples side by side. Another way to discover good plant partners is by studying how they look together in other people's gardens or in magazine and book photos. Don't be ashamed to copy a good idea!

Feathery

Coarse & Bold

Some plants add interest with patterned foliage or flowers: stripes, spots, or splotches of color all provide variety to the basic forms. Some flowers are two-toned, with outer petals of one color and inner ones of another; other plants have lower petals (iris, for example) of one shade and upper ones of another shade. Used in a limited way, these patterns can be an asset. Beware of adding too many plants with patterned foliage or flowers in a small area—it's possible to have too much of a good thing! In that case, you'll end up with a hodge-podge collection instead of a pleasing design.

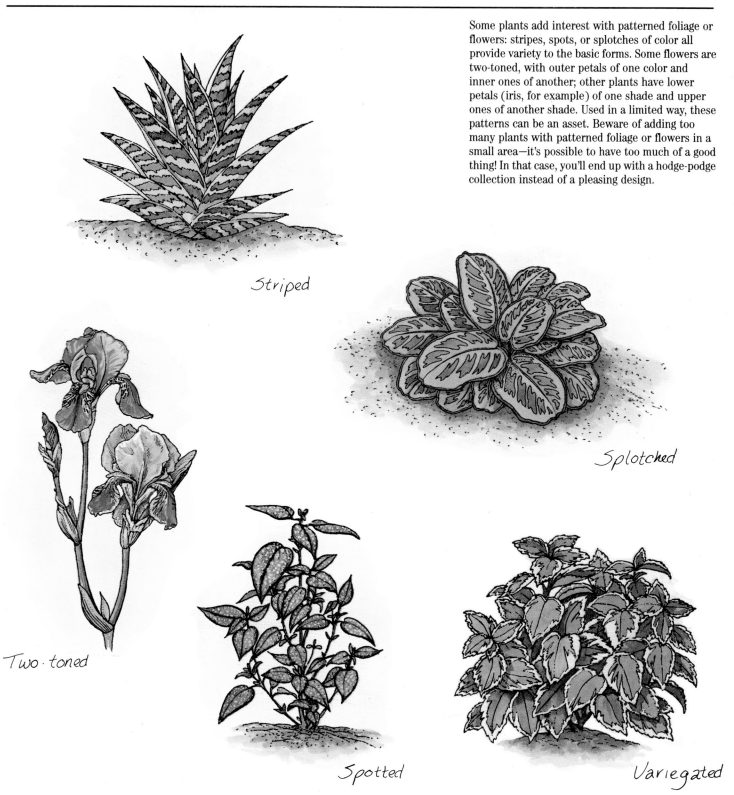

Striped

Splotched

Two-toned

Spotted

Variegated

Selecting Perennials for Color & Characteristics

Perennials of different colors, shapes, and textures can be planted together successfully.

Gardening with perennials is certainly a rewarding undertaking. The plants are very long-lived, versatile, and undemanding. However, if a gardener is planning to use more than one kind of perennial for his planting area, certain factors must be taken into consideration.

Most people prefer to mix different perennial varieties in their gardens, even though it requires a bit more work and planning. Available colors, height of plants, shade or sun preference, soil requirements—all of these factors have to be given attention. Perennial plant textures and forms are two other factors that need to be considered.

Planning a perennial garden in advance is the only way to make sure that a perennial bed is balanced and that the plants work well together in terms of sun or shade, height, soil, form, and texture. For those gardeners who are willing to put in more time and effort, underplanting a perennial garden with bulbs and annuals is another approach that may be considered.

If you list your favorite plants on paper first, noting their available colors and cultural requirements, you're off to a good start. As you narrow down those that work well together, you can actually see a workable garden emerge in front of you. By taking this extra bit of time, you can save yourself from being disappointed later.

The charts that follow are a quick reference for selecting plants for your garden. However, it should be kept in mind that they give only a simplistic first screening. When scanning these lists, you may find many plants that seem appropriate for your garden. However, on further investigation, you'll find that many of them aren't appropriate after all. Use the charts to narrow down the choices; then refer to the more detailed description in the Encyclopedia section beginning on page 92, to identify those best-suited to your climate, soil, and light conditions.

It's important to remember that the "Multicolor" category lists those plants that come in nearly every color range (any perennial that comes in more than three color ranges has been put into this category). Because it contains the most universal and versatile perennials, be sure to use it often when making your selections.

Whether you are a novice or a gardener with many years of planting experience, using a chart with information on color, light, soil, and height can be the difference between a picture-perfect garden and one that just doesn't quite work.

MULTICOLOR FLOWERS

	Dry Soil	Average Soil	Moist Soil	Full Sun	Part Shade	Full Shade	Under 12 Inches	12-24 Inches	Over 24 Inches	Vining
Astilbe			•	•	•			•	•	
Balloon Flower		•	•	•	•			•	•	
Beard Tongue	•			•				•		
Bergamot			•	•					•	
Bergenia, Heartleaf			•		•			•		
Bishop's Hat		•	•		•	•				
Chrysanthemum		•		•				•	•	
Columbine		•		•	•			•	•	
Coralbell		•	•	•	•			•		
Crane's-Bill		•		•	•		•	•		
Daisy, Michaelmas		•		•			•	•	•	
Daylily		•	•	•	•			•	•	
Delphinium		•		•					•	
Fleabane		•		•				•		
Indigo, False	•	•		•	•				•	
Iris		•	•	•			•	•	•	
Knapweed	•	•		•				•	•	
Lungwort			•		•	•		•		
Lupine		•	•	•					•	
Mallow, Rose		•	•	•	•				•	
Peony		•		•	•				•	
Phlox, Garden		•		•	•				•	
Pincushion Flower		•		•	•			•		
Pink		•		•			•	•		
Poppy (Oriental)		•		•					•	
Primrose, Japanese			•		•			•		
Rose, Rock		•		•			•			
Rue, Meadow			•	•	•				•	
Self-heal		•	•	•	•		•			
Speedwell		•		•	•			•		
Spiderwort		•		•	•			•		
Stonecrop	•	•		•				•	•	
Thrift	•			•			•			
Valerian, Red		•		•	•			•	•	
Yarrow	•	•		•	•			•	•	

BLUE TO PURPLE FLOWERS

	Dry Soil	Average Soil	Moist Soil	Full Sun	Part Shade	Full Shade	Under 12 Inches	12-24 Inches	Over 24 Inches	Vining
Ageratum, Hardy			•	•	•			•		
Aster, Stoke's		•		•				•		
Bellflower		•	•	•	•		•	•	•	
Bluestar	•	•		•	•				•	
Bugleweed		•		•	•	•				
Bugloss, Italian		•		•					•	
Bugloss, Siberian			•	•	•	•		•		
Cardinal Flower			•		•				•	
Clematis, Bush		•	•	•	•				•	

BLUE TO PURPLE FLOWERS (continued)

	Dry Soil	Average Soil	Moist Soil	Full Sun	Part Shade	Full Shade	Under 12 Inches	12-24 Inches	Over 24 Inches	Vining
Coneflower, Purple		•		•					•	
Cupid's Dart		•		•				•		
Forget-Me-Not, Chinese	•	•	•	•				•	•	
Holly, Sea	•	•		•				•	•	
Hosta		•	•	•	•	•		•		
Lavender	•	•		•				•		
Lavender, Sea	•	•		•				•		
Lily, Toad		•	•		•				•	
Lily Turf, Big Blue		•		•	•		•	•		
Loosestrife, Purple		•	•	•	•				•	
Periwinkle		•	•	•	•		•			
Rockcress (*Aubrieta*)	•	•		•			•			
Sage, Russian	•	•	•	•					•	
Salvia		•		•					•	
Thistle, Globe		•		•	•				•	

RED FLOWERS

	Dry Soil	Average Soil	Moist Soil	Full Sun	Part Shade	Full Shade	Under 12 Inches	12-24 Inches	Over 24 Inches	Vining
Avens		•	•	•				•		
Blanket Flower		•		•				•		
Cardinal Flower			•		•				•	

PINK TO FUCHSIA FLOWERS

	Dry Soil	Average Soil	Moist Soil	Full Sun	Part Shade	Full Shade	Under 12 Inches	12-24 Inches	Over 24 Inches	Vining
Anemone, Japanese		•	•	•	•				•	
Baby's Breath		•		•			•	•	•	
Blazingstar		•		•					•	
Bleeding Heart			•		•			•		
Butterfly Weed	•	•		•					•	
Coneflower, Purple		•		•					•	
Gas Plant		•	•						•	
Knotweed		•	•	•				•		
Mallow	•	•		•	•				•	
Meadowsweet		•	•	•	•				•	
Nettle, Dead		•			•		•			
Obedient Plant		•	•	•				•	•	
Pea, Perennial	•	•		•	•					•
Poppy, Plume		•		•					•	
Rockcress (*Aubrieta*)	•	•		•		•				
Rock Cress (*Arabis*)	•			•		•				
Rodgersia			•		•				•	
Rose, Christmas			•		•		•			
Soapwort		•		•					•	
Turtlehead			•	•	•				•	

These cultural recommendations are intended to suggest the average conditions over a wide geographical area. It is important to be aware of local requirements.

Sequence of Bloom

Color throughout the growing season is achieved by planning a succession of bloom provided by different species.

Because individual perennials have a limited season of bloom, it's important to know when you can expect each of them to flower. If you want color throughout the entire growing season, you'll need to plan on a succession of bloom provided by different species. With proper planning, it's possible to do this entirely with perennials, even though perennials don't have to stand alone. To obtain summer-long bloom, it's possible to intermix annuals with perennials—the annuals will provide additional flower color from midsummer to late summer.

Also remember that perennial and annual bulbs offer additional summer color possibilities. Gladiolus, tuberoses, fritillarias, resurrection lilies, and, in warm climates, creeping buttercups, can be tucked into small spaces between other plants to provide additional color. Most varied and beautiful are the many hardy lilies that provide an outstanding display of different colors and forms throughout the summer.

Summer isn't the only season when bulbs add beauty to the landscape. All of the spring-flowering bulbs—tulips, daffodils, flowering onions, crocuses, scillas, snowdrops, hyacinths, anemones, etc.—are certainly well known, popular, and easily grown perennial additions to most gardens.

Plant bulbs so the flower stems will be taller than the adjacent plants—this way, their lovely display will be fully visible. After the blooms die, remove the dead flowers in order to direct as much plant energy as possible back into forming large bulbs for next year's growth and blooms. As the flower stems and leaves die back, they'll disappear below the level of adjacent plant foliage and be hidden from view.

When developing your garden plan, avoid clumping all of the plants that bloom at the same time in one part of the garden. Be sure to have a balance of early, mid-season, and late bloomers mixed throughout the planting area.

At first, the idea of intermixing and underplanting may sound too complex. Don't become discouraged. Although it's difficult to plant a well-balanced perennial garden by simply digging holes in the ground and poking plants into them, the job becomes fairly simple if you take the time to draw up a plan on paper in advance. This lets you detect any problems and change them before you ever buy or plant anything. There will probably still be some changes to be made from year to year as you discover new plants you'd like to add, existing plants that you decide to abandon and replace because they never seem to prosper, and others that you feel would look better in a different location.

The Four Seasons
of a Perennials Garden

These four photographs show the same perennials
garden during the four main blooming seasons, with
different plants in flower during each period.

Spring Border: Pinks (*Dianthus* 'Essex Witch'),
bellflowers (*Campanula latifolia* 'Brantwood'),
and Siberian irises (*Iris sibirica* 'Ruffled Velvet').

Early Summer Border: False indigo (*Baptisia*
species) and early daylilies (*Hemerocallis* species).

Late Summer Border: Daylilies (*Hemerocallis*
'Green Flutter'), shasta daisies (*Chrysanthemum* x
superbum), meadowsweet (*Filipendula rubra*),
and purple loosestrife (*Lythrum Salicaria*).

Fall Border: Stonecrop (*Sedum spectabile*),
sunflowers (*Helianthus* x *multiflorus*), Japanese
anemone (*Anemone* species), golden asters
(*Chrysopsis mariana*), wormwood (*Artemisia*
species), and big blue lily turfs (*Liriope Muscari*).

Selecting Perennials by Bloom Date

T his bloom date chart is designed for Zone 7. Bloom time is approximately 10-14 days earlier for each zone south and 10-14 days later for each zone north for each given entry.

EARLY SPRING

February–March

Christmas Rose; Lenten Rose; Hellebore	*Helleborus* species

LATE SPRING

April–May

Avens	*Geum* species
Basket-of-Gold; Goldentuft; Madwort	*Aurinia saxatilis*
Heartleaf Bergenia	*Bergenia cordifolia*
Bishop's Hat; Barrenwort	*Epimedium* species
Bleeding Heart	*Dicentra* species
Bluestar; Blue-Dogbane; Blue-Star-of-Texas	*Amsonia tabernaemontana*
Creeping Buttercup	*Ranunculus repens*
Candytuft	*Iberis sempervirens*
Bush Clematis; Upright Clematis	*Clematis recta*
Columbine	*Aquilegia* species
Coralbell; Alumroot	*Heuchera sanguinea*
Crane's-Bill	*Geranium* species
Painted Daisy	*Chrysanthemum coccineum*
Edelweiss	*Leontopodium alpinum*
Fleabane	*Erigeron hybridus*
Chinese Forget-Me-Not	*Cynoglossum nervosum*
Gas Plant; Burning Bush	*Dictamnus albus*
Globeflower	*Trollius* x *cultorum*
Goat's Beard; Wild Spirea	*Aruncus dioicus*
Goldenstar	*Chrysogonum virginianum*

LATE SPRING

April–May

False Indigo; Wild Indigo	*Baptisia australis*
Iris	*Iris* species
Knotweed; Himalaya Fleece Flower	*Polygonum affine*
Lady's Mantle	*Alchemilla* species
Leopard's-bane	*Doronicum cordatum*
Lungwort; Jerusalem Sage	*Pulmonaria officinalis*
Carolina Lupine; Aaron's Rod	*Thermopsis caroliniana*
Dead Nettle	*Lamium maculatum*
Peony	*Paeonia* species
Periwinkle; Myrtle	*Vinca minor*
Pink; Carnation	*Dianthus* species
Poppy	*Papaver orientale*
Japanese Primrose	*Primula Sieboldii*
Rockcress	*Aubrieta deltoidea*
Rock Cress	*Arabis caucasica*
Meadow Rue	*Thalictrum aquilegifolium*
Sundrop; Evening Primrose	*Oenothera* species
Thrift; Sea Pink	*Armeria maritima*

SUMMER

June–August

Japanese Anemone	*Anemone* species
Golden Aster	*Chrysopsis mariana*
Stoke's Aster	*Stokesia laevis*
Astilbe; Garden Spiraea	*Astilbe* species
Avens	*Geum* species
Baby's Breath	*Gypsophila paniculata*
Balloon Flower	*Platycodon grandiflorus*
Beard Tongue	*Penstemon barbatus*
Bellflower	*Campanula* species
Bergamot; Bee-Balm; Oswego-Tea	*Monarda didyma*
Blanket Flower	*Gaillardia* x *grandiflora*
Blazingstar; Gayfeather	*Liathris* species
Bleeding Heart	*Dicentra* species
Italian Bugloss	*Anchusa azurea*
Creeping Buttercup	*Ranunculus repens*
Butterfly Weed; Milkweed	*Asclepias tuberosa*
Cardinal Flower	*Lobelia Cardinalis*
Cinquefoil	*Potentilla thurberi*
Bush Clematis; Upright Clematis	*Clematis recta*
Black Cohosh	*Cimicifuga racemosa*
Yellow Coneflower; Black-eyed Susan	*Rudbeckia fulgida*
Coralbell, Alumroot	*Heuchera sanguinea*
Coreopsis	*Coreopsis* species
Crane's-Bill	*Geranium* species
Cupid's Dart	*Catananche caerulea*
Michaelmas Daisy	*Aster* species
Painted Daisy	*Chrysanthemum coccineum*

SUMMER

June–August

Shasta Daisy	*Chrysanthemum* x *superbum*
Daylily	*Hemerocallis* species
Delphinium; Larkspur	*Delphinium* species
Pearly Everlasting	*Anaphalis* species
Feverfew	*Chrysanthemum Parthenium*
Fleabane	*Erigeron hybridus*
Chinese Forget-Me-Not	*Cynoglossum nervosum*
Yellow Foxglove	*Digitalis grandiflora*
Gas Plant; Burning Bush	*Dictamnus albus*
Gaura	*Gaura Lindheimeri*
Goat's Beard; Wild Spirea	*Aruncus dioicus*
Goldenrod	*Solidago* hybrids
Feather Reed Grass	*Calamagrostis acutiflora stricta*
Fountain Grass	*Pennisetum alopecuroides*
Sea Holly	*Eryngium* species
Inula	*Inula ensifolia*
Iris	*Iris* species
Knapweed	*Centaurea* species
Ladybells	*Adenophora confusa*
Lavender	*Lavandula angustifolia*
Sea Lavender	*Limonium latifolium*
Ligularia	*Ligularia* species
Blackberry Lily; Leopard Lily	*Belamcanda chinensis*
Big Blue Lily Turf	*Liriope Muscari*
Gooseneck Loosestrife	*Lysimachia clethroides*
Purple Loosestrife	*Lythrum Salicaria*
Lupine	*Thermopsis caroliniana*
Carolina Lupine; Aaron's Rod	*Lupinus polyphyllus*
Mallow	*Malva Alcea*
Rose Mallow; Swamp Mallow	*Hibiscus Moscheutos*
Dead Nettle	*Lamium maculatum*
Sea Oats	*Chasmanthium latifolium*
Obedient Plant; False Dragonhead	*Physostegia virginiana*
Ox-Eye; False Sunflower	*Heliopsis helianthoides*
Perennial Pea; Sweet Pea	*Lathyrus latifolius*
Garden Phlox	*Phlox paniculata*
Pincushion Flower	*Scabiosa caucasica*
Plume Poppy	*Macleaya cordata*
Rodgersia	*Rodgersia aesculifolia*
Rock Rose; Sun Rose; Frostweed	*Helianthemum nummularium*
Russian Sage	*Perovskia* species
Salvia; Meadow Sage	*Salvia* x *superba*
Self-heal	*Prunella Webbiana*
Sneezeweed; Swamp Sunflower	*Helenium autumnale*
Soapweed	*Yucca glauca*
Soapwort; Bouncing Bet	*Saponaria officinalis*
Speedwell	*Veronica spicata*
Spiderwort	*Tradescantia* x *Andersoniana*

SUMMER

June–August

Perennial Sunflower	*Helianthus* x *multiflorus*
Globe Thistle	*Echinops Ritro*
Red Valerian; Jupiter's-Beard	*Centhranthus ruber*
Yellow Waxbell	*Kirengeshoma palmata*
Wormwood	*Artemisia* species
Yarrow	*Achillea* species

FALL

September–Frost

Hardy Ageratum; Mist Flower	*Eupatorium coelestinum*
Japanese Anemone	*Anemone* species
Golden Aster	*Chrysopsis mariana*
Siberian Aster	*Aster* species
Beard Tongue	*Penstemon barbatus*
Bleeding Heart	*Dicentra* species
Boltonia	*Boltonia asteroides*
Chinese Chives; Garlic Chives	*Allium tuberosum*
Chrysanthemum	*Chrysanthemum* species
Bush Clematis; Upright Clematis	*Clematis recta*
Coralbell; Alumroot	*Heuchera sanguinea*
Coreopsis	*Coreopsis* species
Michaelmas Daisy	*Aster* species
Shasta Daisy	*Chrysanthemum maximum*
Feather Reed Grass	*Calamagrostis acutiflora stricta*
Fountain Grass	*Pennisetum alopecuroides*
Maiden Grass	*Miscanthus sinensis* 'Gracillimus'
Zebra Grass	*Miscanthus sinensis* 'Zebrinus'
Gaura	*Gaura Lindheimeri*
Ladybells	*Adenophora confusa*
Toad Lily	*Liriope Muscari*
Big Blue Lily Turf	*Tricyrtis hirta*
Mallow	*Malva Alcea*
Rose Mallow	*Hibiscus Moscheutos*
Obedient Plant; False Dragonhead	*Physostegia virginiana*
Ox-Eye; False Sunflower	*Heliopsis helianthoides*
Sea Oats	*Chasmanthium latifolium*
Russian Sage	*Perovskia* species
Salvia; Meadow Sage	*Salvia* x *superba*
Sneezeweed; Swamp Sunflower	*Helenium autumnale*
Soapwort; Bouncing Bet	*Saponaria officinalis*
Speedwell	*Veronica spicata*
Stonecrop	*Sedum spectabile*
Perennial Sunflower	*Helianthus* x *multiflorus*
Turtlehead; Balmony	*Chelone glabra*
Red Valerian; Jupiter's-Beard	*Centhranthus ruber*
Yellow Waxbell	*Kirengeshoma palmata*
Wormwood	*Artemisia* species

This pleasing garden shows the variety of perennials that can be planted together. The different hues, forms, and textures combine to produce a garden that is soothing to the eye. This garden is truly a perennials oasis.

CHAPTER 2

GETTING YOUR GARDEN OFF TO A GOOD START

Unlike beds for annuals or vegetables, perennial plant beds are not dug up and replanted every year. Once perennials are planted, there will be no need to do more than routine weeding, feeding, cultivation, and mulching for several years.

This chapter contains instructions for proper flower bed preparation, as well as information on the tools you'll need. Strong, healthy plants are better able to survive such difficulties as drought, insect infestations, and diseases. Learn how to get your garden off to a good start. This will almost certainly result in less work in the long run!

Also included is information about how to properly handle pre-grown, potted, and bare-root plants. The hints in these sections will help you to reduce plant loss during the critical transplanting stages. You'll also learn what to look for when selecting plants at the nursery or garden center, so that you can be sure that the plants you buy are in good, healthy condition.

Study the information contained here before laying out and tilling your perennial planting areas or purchasing any plants. You'll find the time spent studying this information in advance will save much future effort.

Groundwork: Turning & Enriching the Earth

Good care of perennials is the key to their success.

I f the results of your soil test indicate a lack of certain nutrients, you should follow the recommendations made by the testing company. If the imbalance is slight, organic fertilizers can be used. When fast results are needed, or if the imbalance of nutrients is great, inorganic fertilizers are the better choice. A combination of both may be a good compromise solution, using the quick-to-feed commercial plant foods first, then following up in subsequent years with the slow-feeding organic fertilizers.

Commercial fertilizer is commonly formulated in some combination of the three major nutrients: nitrogen, phosphorous, and potassium—N, P, K. The numbers featured on each bag represent the percentage of each of these nutrients in the mix. For example, 5-10-5 contains 5 percent nitrogen (N), 10 percent phosphorous (P), and 5 percent potassium (K). A mixture of 10-10-10 contains 10 percent of each. The NPK formula is also listed on each container of organic fertilizer. The percentages of each nutrient are lower in organic fertilizers than in inorganics. Larger amounts of organics are required to achieve the same results.

It's possible to purchase nutrients separately rather than in a three-nutrient mix. These are useful when there's a deficiency in a single nutrient. Consult with your county Cooperative Extension office or garden center if you feel uncertain about solving nutrient deficiency problems.

Adjusting the nutrient and pH levels in your soil will not improve its *consistency*. To correct soil texture will require the addition of one or several "soil conditioners." The most commonly used conditioners are leaf mold, compost, well-rotted cow manure, and peat moss. Vermiculite, perlite, and sand (coarse builder's sand, *never* use beach sand) can also be added, especially when the basic soil is heavy.

After preparing a planting bed, allow the soil to stand unplanted for a week or more. Stir the surface inch or two every three to four days with a rake to eradicate fast-germinating weed seeds. This will make your future weeding chores lighter.

This is also the time to install some kind of mowing strip. Patio squares or slate pieces laid end-to-end at ground level will keep grass and flowers from intermixing. Other options include landscape logs, poured concrete strips, or bricks laid side-by-side on a sand or concrete base. The mowing strip must be deep and wide enough so grass roots cannot tunnel underneath or travel across the top to reach the flower bed, and the top of the strip must not extend above the level of the adjacent lawn.

1 Preparing a Garden Bed

Mark out the new garden area with pegs and string as guides for digging (use a garden hose as a guide for any curved lines). Using a spade or edger, cut through the sod along string lines, skim the sod layer off, then cut back and remove any underlying roots.

2

Thoroughly turn and loosen the soil to about a 6-inch depth, removing rocks as you go. For medium to large areas, use a rototiller for this job (if you don't have one, either rent one or hire someone to do the tilling). For a very small area, use a spade.

3

Smooth the soil surface with an iron rake—do a very rough job, since you'll be redigging the area again. Remove rocks and roots that surface during the raking.

4

Spread on soil additives (compost, moistened peat moss, perlite, fertilizer, etc.) as recommended by your soil test results. Work them in with a tiller or spade—since the upper soil layer is much looser, you'll be able to till more deeply— to a 10- to 12-inch depth this second time. Wait a week or so before planting in order to allow the soil to settle.

Transplanting from Pots

These nursery-grown perennials are well cared for.

Many garden shops and nurseries offer an extensive variety of perennials planted in containers. Whereas in the past there were just a few mail-order specialists from whom the more unusual perennials could be purchased, it's now possible to obtain what you want locally. This allows you to select the individual plants you prefer and to see their condition before you buy.

Potted perennials are offered in a number of sizes from small plants in 3- to 4-inch pots to mature plants in gallon-sized, metal or plastic containers. The small plants are usually only a few months old. In most instances, these will not produce blooms the first season. Those in large containers are often in bloom at the time of purchase and can be expected to quickly become established in their new sites. Smaller plants usually cost less than larger ones; when small plants are priced high, it's because they're rare or exceedingly slow or difficult to propagate. Containerized plants should be planted outdoors as promptly as possible after purchase. The longer they're kept in containers, the more likely they are to dry out and become pot-bound. If you *must* hold plants for a long time prior to planting, place them where they'll be under light shade, and be sure to water them. When you're ready to plant container-grown plants, thoroughly moisten the soil before knocking them out of the pot. Plunge the container into a pail of water to above the pot's rim for a few minutes. Snap off any roots sticking out of the pot bottom. The plant should slide out into your hand. If it doesn't, run a knife blade around the inside of the pot to help release the root ball. If all else fails, break off the pot by knocking it against something solid; in the case of plastic or metal containers, cut them open and peel them off, avoiding damage to the roots as much as is reasonably possible.

Loosen and remove any excess soil from around the roots. Most soil-less mixes will fall away on their own. If the mix adheres to the roots, take away only as much as comes off easily with your fingers. Soil-less mixes dry faster than garden soil, so you want to eliminate what you can without badly disturbing the root ball.

Always place the plant in the ground at the same depth as it was in the pot and provide a water-holding area by forming a soil dam a few inches away from the stem. Transplant in the evening or on a cloudy day; otherwise, provide shade for three to four days by setting an overturned box or a newspaper cone over each plant. Tuck a 2-inch mulch layer around the plants and deep water as needed the first growing season.

Transplanting Potted Plants

1 Submerge potted plants in water before transplanting; this helps the plant to slide out of the container more easily. To avoid damage to the plant top and help keep the root ball intact, spread your hand over the top of the pot with stems and leaves poking out between your fingers. Then turn the pot upside down and gently tap its rim against something solid to loosen the root ball from the sides of the pot. The plant will slide out of the pot into your hand.

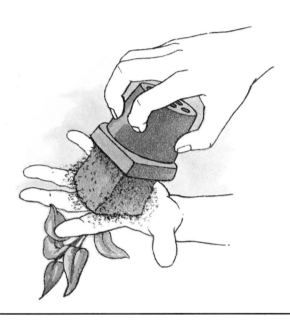

2 If the plant root ball is tightly packed with roots, these should be gently loosened. They need to spread out after planting, rather than continue to grow in a tight mass. If they resist loosening with your fingers, cut up into the sides of the root ball in several places with a sharp knife or scissors, then shake the roots loose a bit more with your fingers before planting. If roots are not tightly packed, skip this step. **Note:** Knock only one plant out at a time to avoid exposing the roots to the drying qualities of air and light.

 3

The plant hole should be somewhat larger in diameter than the root ball and deep enough to allow you to plant at the same depth as the plant was growing in the container. Fan out the loosened roots over a small soil mound in the center of the hole to encourage spreading root growth.

4 Refill the hole with soil, then firm the soil around the plant stem and roots. Create a soil dam around the plant and fill it with water. As the water soaks in, it will help settle the soil and remove any remaining air pockets around the roots—air pockets can cause delicate feeder roots to dry out and die. Lay a 2-inch layer of mulch around the crown and under trailing foliage.

Buying Healthy Plants

Perennials will thrive if they are healthy when planted.

Although most garden centers try very hard to supply healthy plants in peak condition—free of disease and insect infestations—it's still possible for problems to escape their notice. A reputable retailer will certainly replace any plants that you may purchase and find to be sick after getting them home. However, by then the damage of passing the problem on to other plants in your garden may already have been done. It is far better to learn what to look for, so that you can protect yourself as much as possible from this kind of problem!

First and foremost, observe the degree of care or neglect that the plants receive at each nursery or garden center. If plants appear wilted, leaves are sun-scorched, or the soil is bone dry, it's probably not a one-time happening. Each time a plant wilts badly, it loses strength. If the retailer doesn't water regularly and does not provide shade for the more vulnerable and shade-loving plants, it's very likely that the plants will be in a weakened condition when you buy them. This, in turn, makes them more susceptible to disease and insect infestations, because they have less strength with which to survive such problems.

Unless you buy the plants very early in the season before they've gone through many wilting cycles, it's best not to purchase plants from a source where they haven't received proper care. There are many alternative sources where good care is given. Look for strong, vital, healthy new growth, and plants that have been handled properly.

You also want to inspect each plant carefully for signs of infestation. Signs of problems include: stippled holes dotting leaves (leafhoppers); squiggly trails on leaves (leaf miners); extremely fine webs on underside of leaves (red spiders); stickiness on plant stems and leaves (red spiders or aphids); colonies of tiny, soft-bodied bugs on flower buds and growth tips (aphids); ants busily running up and down stems (aphids); whitish fluff that turns sticky if pinched (mealybugs); hard, round or oval, shell-like formations on stems (scale); clouds of tiny white insects rising from the plant when you touch it (white flies); leaf edges chewed (caterpillars); grayish-white powder on leaves (mildew); and plant tips wilted, while lower stems and leaves are not (stem borers). More detailed descriptions of insects and diseases can be found in the next chapter; this list simply provides the primary warning signals to heed when screening plants in the garden center. If you think you see any of these signals, point them out to your retailer. Especially during their busy spring season, it's difficult for retailers to spot the beginning of every possible problem. Good plantsmen will want to take steps to combat an infestation as early as possible.

It's always helpful to be able to see the plants you're buying in advance. If you're unable to find the particular kinds you want, you can be reassured that there are many, very reliable mail-order sources of high-quality perennials. Frequently, these growers are the only source of the newest and less well-known varieties; it would be a shame to miss growing the many beautiful perennials they offer.

How can you identify which companies can be relied upon to provide top quality plants? Probably the best way is to talk to other gardeners to learn which companies have given them consistently good service and quality plants, and which have not. Another is by reading the fine print on the guarantee the company offers; reputable firms will stand behind their product. If wild claims and rave notices are given to every plant listed in their catalog, and the prices at which they're offered are far lower than from any other sources, chances are you're either going to receive an extremely small plant or a close-to-weed variety. In the plant world, you get what you pay for!

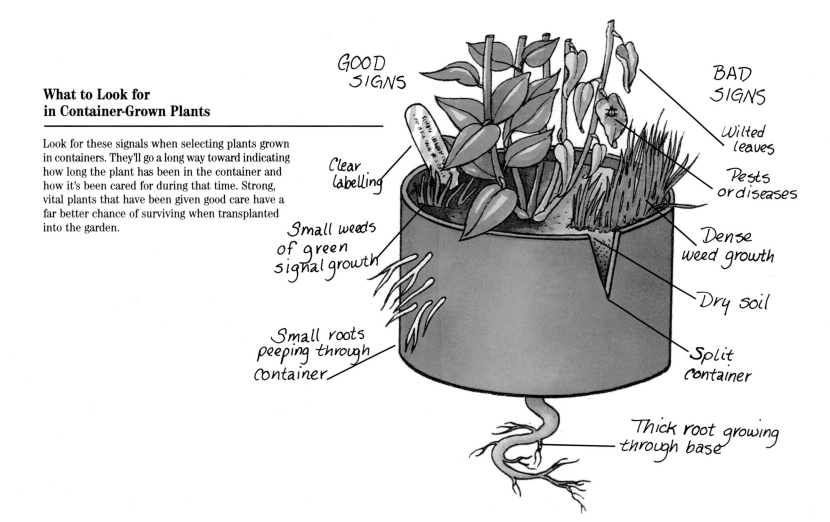

CONTAINER-GROWN PLANT

GOOD SIGNS

BAD SIGNS

Wilted leaves

Pests or diseases

Clear labelling

Small weeds of green signal growth

Dense weed growth

Dry soil

Small roots peeping through container

Split container

Thick root growing through base

What to Look for in Container-Grown Plants

Look for these signals when selecting plants grown in containers. They'll go a long way toward indicating how long the plant has been in the container and how it's been cared for during that time. Strong, vital plants that have been given good care have a far better chance of surviving when transplanted into the garden.

Here is a brief list of mail-order suppliers of perennial plants:

Kurt Bluemel, Inc.
2740 Greene Lane
Baldwin, MD 21013

Canyon Creek Nursery
3527 Dry Creek Road
Oroville, CA 95965

Milaeger's Gardens
4838 Douglas Avenue
Racine, WI 53402

Wayside Gardens
1 Garden Lane
Hodges, SC 29695

Bluestone Perennials, Inc.
7211 Middle Ridge Road
Madison, OH 44057

Carroll Gardens
P.O. Box 310
Westminster, MD 21157

Prairie Nursery
P.O. Box 306
Westfield, WI 53964

White Flower Farm
Route 63
Litchfield, CT 06759

Busse Gardens
Rt. 2 Box 238
Cokato, MN 55321

Holbrook Farm & Nursery
Route 2, Box 223B
Fletcher, NC 28732

Andre Viette Farm & Nursery
Route 1, Box 16
Fishersville, VA 22939

This planting of primroses, bugleweeds, and azaleas requires minimal maintenance. If kept in top condition, these plants will come back each growing season to add color to a garden and to provide it with interesting forms and textures.

GIVE YOUR PERENNIALS LOTS OF CARE

Fortunately, once perennial plantings are established, they require minimal maintenance. That's one of their big advantages: The plants simply keep coming back each growing season for as long as they're kept healthy and vigorous.

This doesn't mean, of course, that no care at all is needed. Those gardeners who have very little time or inclination to work with perennials are advised to select plants that are vigorous and self-sustaining, that don't require staking, are least prone to insect and disease problems, are winter hardy, and survive summer's heat.

None of the jobs you'll do to keep perennials in peak condition requires a great deal of time and energy when taken individually. Some things you'll simply do as you walk along—pause to pull out a stray weed or snap off a dead flower. Chores such as spraying and mulching, which require special preparation or equipment, you can do when you have extra time available.

This chapter provides information on the care techniques used to maintain perennials throughout the entire growing season. Included are tips to ready them for overwintering. Use these tips to keep your perennials in top condition year after year.

Watering, Weeding, & Feeding

Watering hostas will encourage vigorous growth.

I f you feed and water perennials well and keep weeds from intruding on their space, they'll respond with vigorous growth and numerous blooms. Here's how to keep them at their best:

Watering—Water, soil, and sun are the most essential ingredients for plants. It's necessary to water perennials the first season after planting whenever nature doesn't supply enough rain. After the first year, most perennials can sustain themselves without watering, except during exceptionally dry spells.

When watering *is* necessary, always water deeply in order to encourage deep root growth. When only the surface inch or two is moistened, the plant's roots are encouraged to grow primarily in that area. Then, as soon as the soil surface dries, they quickly wilt. Shallow-rooted plants are also not anchored well enough to survive strong winds or winter's freezing and thawing action.

Deep watering is done most easily, and is least wasteful of water, when applied with a soaker hose laid around the plants. Allow water to slowly seep from the hose into the soil over a period of several hours. Dig down into the soil to be sure it has soaked in to a depth of 6 to 8 inches. Don't water again until a bit of soil pinched between your fingers feels nearly dry.

Weeding—Mulching helps retain soil moisture. It also greatly reduces the need for weeding, because the mulch layer inhibits many weed seeds from sprouting. Lay on the mulch to a depth of 2 inches right after planting. As you spread the mulch, take care to lift trailing foliage so it lies on top of the mulch, and be sure to keep space open around each plant's growth center to avoid smothering.

When a mulch is used, only a bit of hand weeding will be required around perennials. However, if for some reason a mulch is not used, hand cultivation of the top 1 inch of soil will be needed frequently throughout the summer to stir up the soil and discourage weed growth. Care must be taken not to damage roots or leave them exposed to sun and air, and not to scratch so deeply that hidden bulbs are damaged.

A third alternative for weed control among perennials is to sprinkle a pre-emergent chemical weed control on the soil between the plants. This should not be used in areas where seeds or young plants are growing; once plants are 4 to 6 inches high, they will not be harmed by these chemicals.

Feeding—Perennials profit from two or three light applications of general fertilizer each summer. Most important is a sidedressing of granular fertilizer each spring as growth starts; one or two additional lighter applications at 3- to 4-week intervals are helpful but not essential.

Use a commercial mixture of 5-10-5 or 10-10-10. If you prefer to use an organic fertilizer, simply apply more heavily, or at more frequent intervals to supply the same level of nutrition to the plants.

Watering with a Soaker Hose

A soaker hose allows water to slowly seep into the soil, allowing deep, thorough watering. At the same time, it applies water directly to the root zone without waste in runoff. It provides the additional advantage of not wetting down the foliage, which in turn cuts down on disease and mildew problems, as well as bending and breakage of plant stems from water weight. Weave the hose through the bed early in the season, leaving the end with the quick-connector attachment near the outside edge. The regular garden hose can then easily be hooked up to it whenever deep watering is needed to supplement nature's supply, and disconnected and stored away between uses.

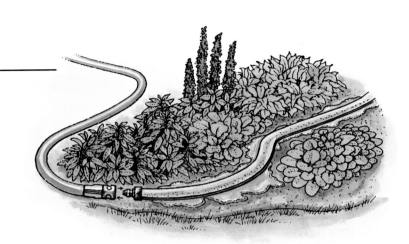

Bubbler Wand for Watering Individual Plants

To water a few individual plants rather than the entire flower bed, a bubbler wand can be connected to the garden hose. This device breaks the pressure of the water as it hits the ground, allowing slow watering without water runoff or erosion of the soil. You can water with a bubbler wand while standing upright; or you can lay it down in an area for a while and let the water soak in, moving it to another section when needed.

Feeding with a Garden Hose Attachment

Another feeding alternative is to add nutrients by way of an attachment to the garden hose. This way, watering and feeding go on simultaneously. This is particularly easy to do if a drip irrigation system or soaker hose is the primary water source. Follow the manufacturer's recommendations regarding the frequency and rate of application.

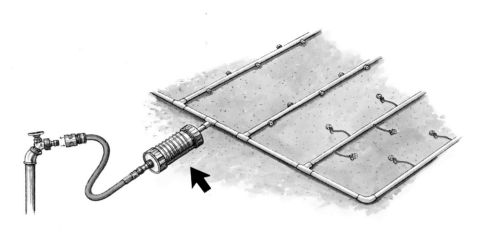

Mulching

A mulch layer on top of the soil keeps down weeds, almost entirely eliminating the need for weeding. It helps retain moisture in the soil, reducing the need for watering, and gives the garden a neat, cared-for appearance. It also evens out soil temperatures, so plants suffer less damage from extremes of heat and cold—it insulates plant roots over winter, allowing them to avoid damage from heaving. Use any mulch material that's readily available and inexpensive in your area: shredded bark, leaves, peanut shells, buckwheat or cocoa bean hulls, pine needles, wood chips—even shredded newspaper.

Hand Weeding

When a mulch is used, little weeding is required— simply pull out the few weeds that are present by hand. Without a mulch, there will be more weeds to control; stir the top 1 to 2 inches of soil with a hand cultivator frequently to kill young weed seedlings as they emerge. Use a weeding tool to root them if they are larger and better established.

Ways to Increase/Control Growth

As has already been described, perennials will flourish when provided with the best possible growing conditions. However, there are a few simple care techniques that will help increase and control their growth.

Pinching Back—To encourage plants to fill out, remove the growth bud at the end of the main stem when the plant is in the rapid growth stage that precedes flower bud formation. Simply pinch out or snap off the last 1 inch or so of the main growing tip. This will redirect the plant's energy from this single shoot to numerous latent side buds—there is a latent growth bud located at the point on the stem where each leaf is attached.

Several days after pinching, you'll see small side shoots pushing from the remaining stem. These will grow into a cluster of stems to replace the original single stem. The plant will be shorter, stockier, and fuller than if no pinching had been done. It will also be neater looking, more compact, and have many more branches on which to produce flowers.

A second pinching can be done two weeks after the first if an even fuller plant is wanted. Pinching is not right for *all* perennials. Among those that respond well to pinching are chrysanthemums and feverfew.

Disbudding—If you want to have each stem produce a single large bloom rather than numerous smaller ones, it's possible to steer all of the plant's energy into one terminal bud by snapping out all side buds along the stem as they appear. Disbudding is often done on peonies, carnations, and oriental poppies.

Deadheading—There are two reasons for removing spent flowers promptly: 1) Once the flower dies, it detracts from the good looks of the garden; and 2) Even though we say it's dead, it's actually very much alive and continues with its growth toward seed production. This process pulls plant energy into the seed head that would otherwise be available for foliage and root production.

Shearing—The abundance of dead flower heads on low-spreading plants is most easily removed by shearing them with grass clippers immediately after they've finished blooming. This shearing of the top few inches will not only speedily dispose of unwanted dead blooms, but will also encourage attractive new foliage growth.

Simple care techniques make perennials look this full and healthy.

Pruning Back—Occasionally, it becomes necessary to cut back growth in order to keep a plant from drowning out neighboring plants. Cut back to a side bud or shoot that is headed in the direction you want future growth to go. In the case of grasses and other plants that grow from a ground level central crown, cut back the entire stem.

Increasing Growth Through Pinching

Pinching out the growth tip early in the season encourages plants such as chrysanthemums and asters to push out multiple side shoots. This creates a fuller and more spreading plant with many more flower buds than if it were left unpinched. Beware of waiting too late in the season before pinching; it must be done before the plant starts forming buds—usually by the 4th of July.

Deadheading

Deadheading, or the removal of dead flower heads, should be done soon after the flower dies so no plant energy is wasted on seed formation. Cut the flower off at a point just above a side shoot or branch, or down to the ground if the plant pushes flowers directly from the root crown. Cluster flowers will look fresh and attractive longer if the individual florets are snapped out of the group as they die.

Shearing Low-Spreading Plants

Some perennials can be sheared to remove dead flowers. This is particularly useful on low-spreading plants such as basket-of-gold, thyme, and candytuft, which are literally covered with flowers each spring. Shearing should be done immediately after the flowers have faded to encourage the plant to fill out and look attractive the rest of the season as well as to produce abundant blooms the following year.

Thinning

Some plants such as phlox, aster, and delphinium produce so much foliage that none of it blooms well. By thinning out all but a few of the strongest shoots in early spring, it's possible to channel the plant energy into these to produce nice, large blooms. To do this, use a sharp knife, scissors, or hand pruners to cut out all but the sturdiest half dozen stems when they reach a height of 4 to 6 inches. The remaining stalks will quickly fill in the spaces and prosper without the excess competition.

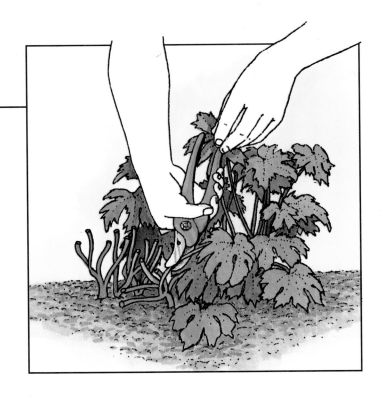

Staking Garden Plants

Many perennials are sturdy and self-supporting and do not require any special staking to keep them looking good. However, plants with flower clusters on top of tall slender stems, such as lilies and delphiniums, may flop over when there are strong winds or heavy rains. Another group that sometimes requires support to keep flower heads visible are those with weak stems, which will either bend over or break off when the weight of their leaves and blooms becomes too great. Some varieties of peonies, bearded irises, and carnations are known to have these problems.

Often plants gain enough support when a sort of corral is placed around them. The plant stems lean out against the metal or string sides of the corral instead of flopping down to the ground.

Another simple type of support consists of poking many-branched pieces of brush into the ground beside the plants. These form a network of twigs through which the plants can grow and against which they can lean for support. For greater support, the tops of these branches can be bent over to form an interlaced network.

The above support systems work well for plants with a spreading growth habit. For those that produce tall, single spikes, a third staking method is suitable. Two or three inches from the plant stem, poke a wooden or bamboo stake into the ground. Push it in deeply enough so it's solidly secure. Loosely tie each plant stem to this central stake every 6 inches along the stem's height. The topmost tie should be just below the flower bud cluster. To keep the ties from sliding down, first form a half-granny knot around the stake, then a full-granny knot around the plant stem.

Sometimes tying plants seems a nuisance, although it really only takes a few minutes to do. But if those plants that need it aren't tied, they'll either bend over, becoming impossible to see; or they'll snap off, wilt, and die. If you aren't willing to stake your plants, then don't grow those that require it. Select easier care varieties instead—there are many with sturdy growth habits that don't need staking.

Of course, if it happens that your favorite plant is one that needs staking, you'll probably conclude you like it enough to give it this bit of extra care in return for the pleasure and beauty it will provide.

This delphinium will grow through these support branches.

Brush Thicket Staking

A simple, no-cost plant support for fine stemmed perennials can be made by poking the stems of well-branched brush into the ground around the plants in early spring. The plants' stems simply lean against the twigs for support, without any tying. Even more support can be gained from this brush thicket if the tops are bent over and interwoven. When the perennial is full grown, trim brush tops so they'll be completely hidden by the perennial foliage and flowers.

Corral Staking

Another good way to hold clumps of stems upright is by inserting four or more plant stakes around each plant. Tie a string around one stake, then wrap it one turn around each of the other stakes and back to the starter stake. For a large clump, run strings diagonally across within the corral that has been formed to provide even more of a support network. Several tiers of string, spaced 4 to 6 inches apart, may be needed for tall plants. The flower heads should float 6 to 8 inches above the top tier of strings.

L-Shaped Metal Stakes

A more expensive but easier to install corral can be made from L-shaped metal stakes sold especially for this purpose. These stakes hook together quickly to make whatever size is needed. These can be used year after year once the initial investment is made. String can be diagonally cross-woven between these stakes if more support is needed.

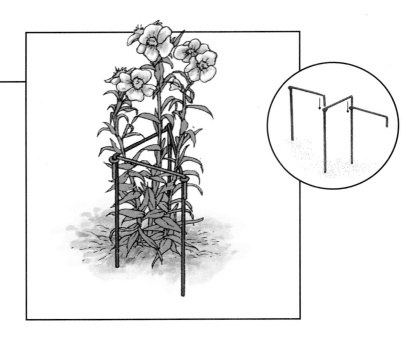

Individual Staking

Those plants that have tall individual stems, such as delphinium and lilies, are best staked individually. Push a tall stake deeply into the soil about 6 inches out from the stem base so it's firmly anchored. Tie the string to the stake first with a half-granny knot, then around the plant stem with a full-granny knot. Leave 1 inch or more of slack between the stake and the stem. As the plant grows taller, add ties further up the stalk—6 to 8 inches apart. The topmost tie should be located at the base of the flower spike.

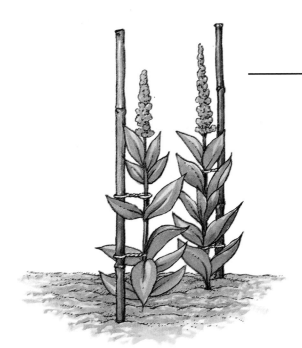

Woven Wire Support

A plant support made from woven wire that is coated with green plastic is inconspicuous and effective. Supports can be either dome-shaped or an open topped circle. Placed over plants in early spring, they support the plants as the shoots grow up through them, ultimately covering them completely.

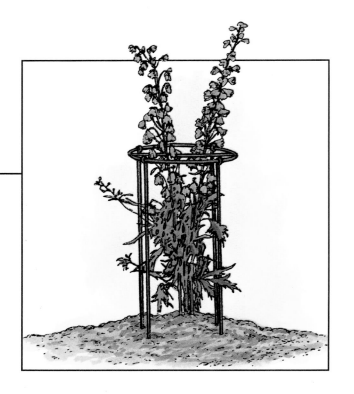

Pests & Other Problems

Healthy-looking plants are truly a gardener's reward.

The following lists are designed to help you identify the most common garden pests and diseases. Each insect, animal, and disease that perennials are susceptible to is presented in column format with a write-up of the most common symptoms and a color picture of the cause and the appearance of the affected plants. Also included are brief recommendations for the cure and a listing of what plants are most susceptible to each particular problem. However, if you feel even slightly uncertain about what may be causing damage to your plants, it is advisable that you take a specimen to your local garden shop or your county Cooperative Extension office to have it identified. Early and correct detection is the key to controlling these problems successfully. If you catch the problem when it first appears, chances are you will be able to get rid of it quickly and thoroughly.

Once you know what your problem is, you'll need to decide how to control it. When an infestation is slight, it's often possible to simply remove the sick plants or individual insects. For a heavy infestation, you'll probably need to turn to chemical insecticides or fungicides. Our charts present both forms of treatment, distinguishing which are organic and which are inorganic.

Just remember to follow the manufacturer's instructions precisely, and to read and follow any cautions on the package label. Apply these chemicals as directed and only when they're absolutely necessary. When people spray or dust with the attitude that "more is better"—whether the plants need it or not—excessive poisons become a possibility.

One final note: New biological and chemical controls are continually being developed. Those listed here are current at the time of this writing, but more effective new ones may well be discovered in the future. Therefore, it is very important to correctly identify your pest or disease problem and to consult with your local nursery or garden center. They can recommend the best available product for controlling that particular problem.

INSECTS AND ANIMALS

SYMPTOM	CAUSE	CURE	PLANTS
Cluster of small, soft-bodied insects on buds and growth tips (gray, black, pink, or green in color); sticky secretions may be evident	*Aphids*	Spray with rotenone or malathion[1] in evening.	Chrysanthemum Shasta Daisy Delphinium Lupine
Leaves chewed away; hard-shelled beetles on plant and burrowed into flowers	*Beetles of various kinds*	Spray with rotenone or Sevin*[1]; pick by hand and destroy.	Chrysanthemum Hollyhock Mallow
Growth tips wilted; small hole in plant stem at point where wilting begins	*Borers*	Snap off at level of hole, dig out borer and destroy. Spray with endosulfan[1], pyrethrum, or rotenone.	Dahlia Delphinium Hollyhock Iris
Leaves and flowers chewed away; caterpillars on plant	*Caterpillars of various kinds & sizes*	Pick off by hand and destroy; or spray with pyrethrum, malathion[1], or *Bacillus thuringiensis*.	Butterfly Weed Chrysanthemum Mallow Yarrow
Leaves and stems chewed; insects hopping and flying	*Grasshoppers*	Spray with Sevin*[1]. Pick off by hand.	Aster Yellow Coneflower Ornamental Grasses
Leaves peppered with small, round holes; small, triangular-shaped bugs seen when disturbed	*Leaf Hoppers*	Spray with malathion[1] or methoxychlor[1]; dust with diatomaceous earth.	Aster Chrysanthemum Coreopsis Pincushion Flower
Leaves "painted" with whitish, curling trails	*Leaf Miners*	Spray with malathion[1]; remove and destroy badly infested leaves.	Columbine Shasta Daisy Pink Hollyhock

[1] = Inorganic treatment.
* = Copyrighted brand name.

Note: Consult your Cooperative Extension Office for approved pesticides for ornamental plants.

SYMPTOM	CAUSE	CURE	PLANTS
Plants entirely gone or eaten down to small stubs; evidence of footprints or droppings	*Rabbits or Deer*	Spray with Hinder*[1]; fence out rabbits with 3′ high chicken wire or other close-woven fencing.	Lily Flowers
Silvery slime trails over soil and plants; soft sticky slugs on plants after dark (check with flashlight); holes eaten in leaves	*Slugs and Snails*	Set out shallow containers of beer; set out metaldehyde slug bait[1]; pick by hand after dark or on dark days.	Daylily Hollyhock Hosta Phlox Moss Pink Primrose
Leaves yellowing with speckled look; fine spider webs on backs of leaves and at point where leaves attach to stem; very tiny bugs on backs of leaves	*Spider Mites*	Spray with a miticide[1] from underneath to hit backs of leaves; wash or spray with soapy water.	Bush Clematis Yellow Coneflower Daylily Primrose
Small glob of white bubbles on plant stem or leaves; small insect hidden inside	*Spittlebugs*	Ignore unless very pervasive; spray with malathion[1]; wash off repeatedly with water from hose.	Chrysanthemum Feverfew Myrtle Oriental Poppy
Brown or white flecks on plant leaves	*Thrips*	Spray with malathion[1] or dust with sulfur.	Daylily Torch Lily
Cloud of tiny white flies fluttering around plant	*White Flies*	Spray with malathion[1] or diazinon[1]; use yellow sticky traps.	Aster Mallow Primrose

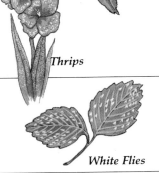

[1] = Inorganic treatment.
* = Copyrighted brand name.

Note: Consult your Cooperative Extension Office for approved pesticides for ornamental plants.

(continued)

DISEASES

SYMPTOM	CAUSE	CURE	PLANTS
Leaves become mottled, curl, and shrivel; plants become deformed	*Blights and Viruses*	Remove and destroy plants; buy blight-resistant strains; do not smoke; wash hands before handling plants.	Japanese Anemone Lupine Peony
Newly sprouted seedlings fall over and die	*Damping Off*	Start seeds in sterile soil mix. Dust seeds with Captan*[1] before planting.	All plants
Round, dusty brown or black spots on leaves; leaves drop from plant	*Leaf Spot*	Remove badly diseased leaves and destroy; spray with benomyl[1] or zineb[1].	Chrysanthemum Iris Phlox
Lower leaves and stems turn grayish and look slightly wilted	*Powdery Mildew*	Increase air circulation; spray with benomyl[1] or sulfur.	Aster Delphinium Phlox Boltonia
Orange or reddish-brown raised dots form on backs of leaves; leaves look wilted	*Rust*	Increase air circulation; keep foliage dry; buy rust-resistant varieties; spray with ferbam[1] or zineb[1]; spray flowers with sulfur or benomyl.	Hollyhock Yarrow
Leaves wilt and turn yellow; entire plant shuts down and dies	*Wilt*	Remove infected plants and destroy; buy wilt-resistant varieties.	Aster Dahlia

[1] = Inorganic treatment.
* = Copyrighted brand name.

Note: Consult your Cooperative Extension Office for approved pesticides for ornamental plants.

Preparing for Winter

Using mulch protects plants from the ravages of winter.

Once early frost hits, you'll find that the top growth will die back on most perennials. When this occurs, use hand pruners to cut off the dead stems, leaving only the bottom 2 to 3 inches. Varieties such as mountain pink and stonecrop, which don't die down, should *not* be cut back.

These cutoff stalks as well as any fallen leaves, flowers, and other garden debris should be removed from the beds and disposed of at this time. Add them to your compost pile if you have one, burn them, or put them into the rubbish bin. This will get rid of any insects or diseases.

Continue deep watering perennials until the ground has solidly frozen. If plants go into winter in a dry condition, they're likely to suffer badly—even die—from winter sun and winds.

In those sections of the country that are warm, no further winter protection is needed. The same is true of the most northern areas, where a deep snow cover protects plants from sun and wind drying as well as from soil temperature fluctuations. It's in those intermediate zones, where snow cover comes and goes and air temperature changes erratically above and below freezing levels that perennials suffer badly from winter damage. In these areas, a protective layer should be laid over the plants and surrounding soil once the ground becomes frozen hard—the idea here is to keep the soil and plants *cold* throughout the winter.

Use whatever is available to provide this protective layer. Saltmarsh hay (difficult to find nowadays and expensive), pine needles, straw, shredded leaves, or evergreen boughs are all good alternatives. This protection should be removed as soon as the frost has left the ground and the lawn feels squishy underfoot. If you've used evergreen branches, remove and discard them; the other protective alternatives can remain as mulching around the plants, if desired. However, they should be removed from the top and drawn back away from the crowns. Usually the mulch will have settled and decomposed over winter so that only 3 to 4 inches remain. If the mulch layer is deeper than this, take off the excess and store it for later use. Bulbs planted under the mulch will be able to poke up through it.

Not all perennials require winter protection. Many old standbys survive very well without any special winter care. Among these are bearded and Siberian iris, peony, coreopsis, aster, columbine, hosta, phlox, evening primrose, and pink bleeding heart.

Plants standing in water from winter thaws is another problem to avoid. When you set the plants in the ground, be sure that the crowns are at or very slightly above ground level. Then, in the early fall, level out any water-holding dams you may have had around the plants. If these are left in place, you run the risk of losing the plants to rot during the winter. Those most susceptible to this problem include delphinium, foxglove, and coralbells. It isn't a good situation for any perennials other than those that enjoy having "wet feet." (See Chapter 5 for more on this special group.)

As you study the plant descriptions and cultural notes in the encyclopedia section, you'll see that a reference to hardiness zones is given for each plant listed. This indicates the coldest winter temperatures that plants can normally be expected to survive without difficulty. Catalogs also list the hardiness zones for plants they're offering; be guided by these.

Naturally, there are temperature variations within a hardiness zone; towns only ten miles apart often experience a temperature difference of ten degrees or more. Different sections of a single garden can vary, too—some parts are sheltered, while cold air always drains or settles in certain areas. Therefore, you need to judge whether *your* local conditions are colder or warmer than the averages given for your zone, and make your selections accordingly. By placing less hardy plants in a spot that is sheltered and faces south, you may be able to grow some varieties that wouldn't otherwise survive in your yard. In general, it's a good idea to select from those that are considered hardy in your own or colder zones.

Cutting Back Stems After Frost

After the first hard frost has killed back the leaves of perennials, use hand pruners to cut the stems back to about 3 inches from the ground. Dispose of the stems and leaves by composting or, if there have been infestations of disease and insects, by burning. Sprinkle a handful of bonemeal around each plant for slow feeding over winter.

Applying a Winter Mulch

Once the ground is frozen hard, a winter mulch layer should be used. Choose a light and loose mulch—one that will allow air and water to pass through easily. Non-matting leaves, such as oak, and evergreen boughs (a great recycling use for your Christmas tree!) are two excellent choices. This mulch will keep the ground cold during winter thaws, thus reducing the likelihood of heaving. It will also reduce the possibility of windburn and sunburn when there is no protective snow layer. Remove this winter mulch as soon as frost has left the ground in very early spring.

Protecting Perennials in Winter

Perennials that are marginally hardy in your zone can sometimes be given adequate extra protection to survive. Wood or wire frames covered with burlap can be set over such plants after the protective winter mulch layer has been applied. Polystyrene cones, designed to protect roses over winter, can be used in this same manner.

Shredded Leaves as Mulch

Shredded leaves are an excellent and easy way to obtain mulch. Once shredded, any type of leaves can be used. Shred them with a shredder/chipper, or run your rotary lawn mower over a mound of them several times, blowing the leaves back toward themselves each time. A 6- to 8-inch layer around the plants, with just the growth crown left uncovered, works well. By spring, the bottom layer will have broken down into nourishing humus; any excess mulch can be removed.

Maintaining Perennials Month by Month

Caring for perennials is a year-round chore.

T he following list includes the various gardening tasks to be done each year. *When* they should be done depends on the climate in your area. Our month-by-month chart indicates when each task should be performed in the different hardiness zones in North America. Because conditions can differ within a zone and dates of first and last freezes of the season vary each year, these are only approximate guides. But they will provide you with a general outline for your garden year. One additional task—that of making notes for future years—should actually be carried out throughout the season. Be sure not to forget it just because it isn't on the list!

Tasks to be Done	Zones 1–3	Zones 4–5	Zones 6–7	Zones 8–10
1—Check and add to winter mulch layer if it has become thin; lay evergreen boughs (if available from Christmas tree) as additional winter protection	JAN	JAN	JAN	
2—Work on garden plan changes for coming season	NOV/DEC/ JAN/FEB	DEC/JAN/FEB	JAN/FEB	JAN
3—Study perennial catalogs and order for coming season	JAN/FEB/ MAR/APR	JAN/FEB/ MAR/APR	JAN/FEB/ MAR/APR	DEC/JAN/FEB
4—Start perennial seeds in seed trays indoors under lights*	MAR/APR	FEB/MAR/APR	JAN/FEB/ MAR/APR	JAN/FEB
5—Water perennial beds if weather is dry	APR/MAY/ JUNE/JULY	APR/MAY/JUNE/ JULY/AUG	JAN/FEB/MAR/ APR/MAY/JUNE/ JULY/AUG/SEPT	JAN/FEB/MAR/ APR/MAY/JUNE/ JULY/AUG/SEPT/ OCT/NOV/DEC
6—Remove top layer of winter mulch when frost leaves ground	MAY	APR	APR	JAN
7—Plant bare-root perennials	MAY	APR	APR	JAN/FEB/MAR
8—Dig and divide summer- and fall-blooming perennials	MAY	APR	APR	FEB/MAR
9—Plant bare-root and container-grown plants	MAY	MAY/JUNE	APR/MAY/JUNE	FEB/MAR
10—Sow perennial seeds outdoors**	MAY	MAY/JUNE	APR/MAY/JUNE	FEB/MAR/APR
11—Lay out and prepare new perennial beds for planting	MAY	MAY/JUNE	APR/MAY/JUNE	FEB/MAR/APR/ NOV/DEC
12—Fertilize with complete fertilizer	MAY	MAY/JUNE	APR/MAY/JUNE	FEB/MAR/APR
13—Thin new growth as needed	MAY	MAY/JUNE	APR/MAY/JUNE	FEB/MAR/APR

Tasks to be Done	Zones 1–3	Zones 4–5	Zones 6–7	Zones 8–10
14—Weed as necessary	MAY/JUNE/ JULY/AUG	MAY/JUNE/JULY/ AUG/SEPT	APR/MAY/JUNE/ JULY/AUG/ SEPT/OCT	MAR/APR/MAY/ JUNE/JULY/ AUG/SEPT
15—Check and treat for insects and diseases	MAY/JUNE/ JULY/AUG	MAY/JUNE/JULY/ AUG/SEPT	APR/MAY/JUNE/ JULY/AUG/ SEPT/OCT	MAR/APR/MAY/ JUNE/JULY/ AUG/SEPT
16—Transplant seedlings from seed tray when first true leaves appear*	APR/MAY	APR/MAY/JUNE	APR/MAY/JUNE	MAR
17—Feed seedlings with water-soluble fertilizer every two weeks*	APR/MAY	APR/MAY/JUNE	APR/MAY/JUNE	
18—Harden off seedlings prior to planting out*	MAY	MAY/JUNE	APR/MAY/JUNE	APR
19—Remove dried foliage and seed heads from ornamental grasses	MAY	MAY/JUNE	APR/MAY/JUNE	APR
20—Set out hardened-off seedlings*	JUNE	MAY/JUNE	MAY/JUNE	APR
21—Set up plant supports as needed	JUNE	MAY/JUNE	MAY/JUNE	APR
22—Apply summer mulch	JUNE	MAY/JUNE	MAY/JUNE	APR
23—Remove dead flowers as necessary	JUNE/JULY	JUNE/JULY/AUG	MAY/JUNE/JULY/ AUG/SEPT	MAY/JUNE/JULY/ AUG/SEPT
24—Pinch mums every two weeks until July 4	JUNE	JUNE	JUNE	MAY/JUNE
25—Tie staked plants as needed	JULY	JULY/AUG	JULY/AUG/SEPT	MAY/JUNE/JULY/ AUG/SEPT
26—Divide and replant oriental poppies, bleeding hearts, etc.	JULY	JULY/AUG	JULY/AUG/SEPT	JULY/AUG/SEPT
27—Take root cuttings and stem cuttings	JULY	JULY/AUG	JULY/AUG/SEPT	JULY/AUG/SEPT
28—Sow seeds outside for flowering next year**	JULY	JULY/AUG	JULY/AUG/SEPT	JULY/AUG/SEPT/ OCT/NOV/DEC
29—Water if conditions are dry, but in reduced amounts to get ready for winter	AUG/SEPT/OCT	SEPT/OCT/NOV	OCT/NOV/DEC	OCT
30—Divide and replant spring- and summer-flowering plants	AUG	SEPT	OCT	OCT
31—Cut tops back after frost has killed them	AUG	SEPT	OCT	
32—Transplant summer seedlings to cold frame**	AUG	SEPT	OCT	
33—Clean up and dispose of garden debris	AUG	SEPT	OCT	NOV
34—Drain and store hoses	SEPT	OCT	NOV	
35—Clean and store garden tools	SEPT	OCT	NOV/DEC	
36—Apply winter mulch when ground is frozen hard	OCT	NOV	DEC	
37—Plant spring-blooming perennials			DEC	OCT/NOV

* —Instructions apply only if starting seeds indoors
** —Instructions apply only if starting seeds outdoors

The purple loosestrife (Lythrum salicaria) in the foreground is one of the many perennials that can be propagated by division. The possibility of creating several plants from one is what makes perennials planting so rewarding.

CHAPTER 4

THE MAGIC OF PROPAGATING NEW PLANTS

There are several different ways in which new plants can be propagated. Most home gardeners become involved in propagation of perennials when some of their plants become too large. They need to dig up these plants and divide them, replanting a small portion later. What happens to the rest of the clump? Sometimes it's simply discarded, but frequently it's replanted elsewhere or passed on to another gardener. As one plant becomes several, *vegetative* propagation has taken place.

Another common form of propagation home gardeners may become involved in is starting plants from *seed*. This occurs when you're unable to find a source for a plant you want. However, not all perennials can be grown true to variety from seed; many *must* be grown from pieces of the parent plant. In these cases, you cultivate pieces of stems or roots and produce new plants from them. A third method of propagation is called *tissue culture* or micropropagation. Many nurseries are now using it to supply inexpensive disease-free plants.

This chapter contains information to help home gardeners successfully start plants from seed, from stem and root cuttings, and by various methods of division.

Starting from Seed

A field of blooming flowers is a treat for the observer.

Perennials can be started from seed indoors during the winter months, or directly in the garden during the growing season. Those started indoors in advance of the growing season will often bloom during their first season in the garden; those started outdoors probably will not.

Outdoor planting can be done almost any time of the year, although in colder climates seeds started in early fall may not develop deep enough roots to survive the winter. Generally, seed starting in spring and early summer is more successful.

Seedbeds should be of a good light loam with moist peat moss or other humus mixed in. They should be located in light shade; if this is not possible, some shading should be provided for the first few weeks after planting. When starting small amounts of seed, a good approach is to sow them in shallow boxes filled with seed starter mix, just as you would if starting them indoors (this sterile soil-less mix eliminates the problem of losing young seedlings to disease or to crowding out by weeds), and placing the boxes in a location where they receive plenty of light but little direct sun.

Sprouting plants will first unfold their seed leaves; within these will be the growth bud for producing their true leaves. When the young seedlings reach the stage where they have their first set of true leaves, they're ready to be carefully transplanted to individual clay, plastic, or peat pots. When they become large enough to survive without special care, they're ready to be planted permanently into the garden.

When starting seeds indoors, it's often difficult to provide enough natural light for them to thrive. As a result, they become leggy and weak. It's easy to avoid this problem by installing grow lights over the plants. Grow lights are special fluorescent tubes that provide the full spectrum of light necessary for good plant growth; they're only slightly more expensive than regular fluorescent lights and can be obtained at most garden shops.

Use a regular fluorescent fixture and hang it in a way that will allow you to easily raise and lower it—ideally, it should be kept 6 to 8 inches above the tops of the plants at all times. Seedlings do best with 16 to 18 hours of light each day; the easiest way to consistently provide this is by plugging the grow light fixture into a simple on-off lamp timer. Remember that although you want to extend the day length, plants also require some hours of darkness in each 24-hour cycle.

Perennial seeds sprout and grow best at a temperature of about 70° F. Water them with lukewarm rather than ice cold water—it's less shocking and helps the seeds thrive. Be sure to keep the planting mix moist, but avoid having it continuously soaking wet; young plants can drown just as easily as they can die from drying out. Once the seeds have sprouted and seedlings have several sets of true leaves, care regarding watering can relax; it's from the time of planting and during the time of sprouting that seedlings are most vulnerable to improper watering.

Planting Seeds

A seedbed for starting perennials should be raked smooth and have all dirt clumps broken so that a fine, even surface is formed. Mark rows with tautly pulled string between stakes, then dig shallow furrows using the side of a trowel or a thin board. Use the string as a guide. Furrows should vary in depth according to seed size—they should be about three times the size of the seed to be planted.

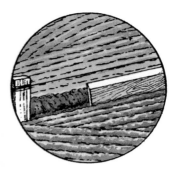

2 Drop individual seeds into the furrow, spacing them ¼ to ½ inch apart. Cover them with very fine, sifted soil or with seed starting mix purchased from a garden supplier—this mix is inert and therefore free of both competing weed seeds and molds or diseases. Since it is very lightweight, tiny seedlings push through it easily. Cover the seeds to a depth of two to three times their diameter. Very fine seeds require no covering.

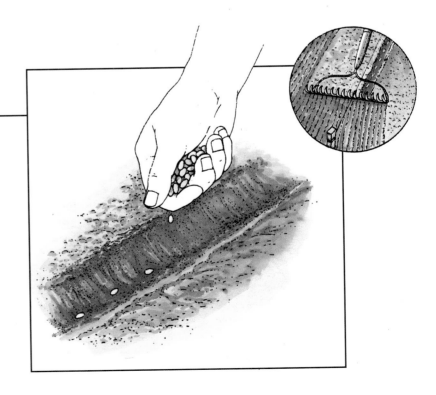

Starting Seeds in a Greenhouse

Those who have a greenhouse available will have plenty of space for growing perennials to sufficient size. You'll still need to supply adequate hours of light for them to grow well—this may mean extending the daylight artificially with grow lights during the shortest days of the year for those living in northern climates.

Hardening off Seedlings

Potted or boxed seedlings should be hardened off for a week or so before transplanting into the garden. This can be done by carrying them outside and leaving them there for a longer time each day before bringing them in overnight. Start by having them outside only one hour, increase to two hours, then four hours, then six hours, etc. This will wean them away from the indoor, hothouselike growing conditions without setting them back from shock. Once the plants have been hardened off in this way, follow planting instructions for container-grown plants.

Starting Stem & Root Cuttings

Oriental poppies can be propagated by root cuttings.

Many perennials cannot be grown from seed because the plants that result will not be exactly like the parent plant. Instead, these perennials must be propagated asexually—this is known as vegetative reproduction.

One way of doing this is by taking pieces of plant stems or roots and growing them into new plants. Gardeners call these pieces *cuttings*. Not all perennials will generate whole new plants from pieces of themselves, although many do this easily.

Stem Cuttings—Stem cuttings should be taken from the active growing tips of the plant. Cuttings should be between 3 and 6 inches in length, and removed from the parent plant in the evening or in early morning when they're in peak condition. Use only healthy plants that are free from insects and diseases and are in an active growing stage.

Gather cuttings for only five minutes, bringing them indoors to process immediately. This will cut down on the possibility of wilting and the energy loss that accompanies it. After one batch of cuttings has been completed, you can gather additional batches, preparing each and inserting the cuttings into the rooting medium before picking a new group.

Rooting hormone powders, though not absolutely essential, do speed up the rooting process and generally help produce a higher percentage of successful "takes." They're long lasting and inexpensive; the smallest packet is all you'll need for hundreds of cuttings.

A rooting medium must provide good drainage and air circulation. At the same time, it must supply support to the plant stems and enough compaction to keep the stems moist. Coarse sand is the traditional rooting medium, but most growers today use some combination of sand, vermiculite, perlite, and peat moss. A mix of perlite combined with an equal amount of either peat moss or vermiculite provides good drainage and moisture retention capability.

Always make a hole first before inserting the prepared cutting into the medium. Firm the medium around the stem. Once all the cuttings are inserted, water them to help them settle into the medium, covering them with a plastic bag to form a tent. The cutting leaves should not come in contact with the plastic. If they do, this is a prime environment for rot that will kill the cuttings. To avoid this problem, insert stakes in the medium in such a way that they will hold the plastic away from the cuttings.

Place this tent in a location where the cuttings will receive good light but no direct sun; keep the medium moist but not wet. The temperature should be about 70° F. Check for roots by gently lifting a cutting from the rooting medium. When roots are ¼-inch long, transplant them into small pots filled with potting mix and grow them until they're sturdy enough to plant outdoors.

Root Cuttings—For just two or three root cuttings, simply dig down beside the parent plant and cut off one or two roots with a knife or hand pruners. For a larger number of root cuttings, dig up the parent plant and trim off all of the side roots. Discard the parent plant, or trim the top back heavily and replant it.

For best results, root cuttings should be taken in early spring (except for oriental poppies, which seem to do better if cuttings are taken in the fall). To help identify the top of the cutting (that part closest to the plant's main root or crown) from the bottom, make cuts straight across the top end and a slanted cut at the bottom end of each segment. Cut fine roots into 1-inch lengths; fleshy ones into 1½- to 2-inch pieces.

Cuttings of fine roots can be scattered horizontally over the surface of the rooting medium (rich sandy loam is best) and covered with about ½ inch of soil or sand. Fleshy roots are planted upright in the medium, 2 to 3 inches apart, with the top ¼ inch of the cutting sticking out of the ground.

Unlike stem cuttings that root within weeks, root cuttings are slow to generate new top growth. Keep them in a sunny location out of direct sun, and continue to water them whenever the rooting medium begins to dry.

How to Start Perennials from Stem Cuttings

1 Cut 3- to 6-inch growth tips from the parent plant with a small, sharp knife. Make a clean, slanted cut just above a leaf node, side shoot, or growth bud. The parent plant should be in a stage of active growth with young and succulent stems. If the stems are woody and difficult to cut, try recutting closer to the tip. Bring cuttings indoors immediately and recut them just below the bottom node. Use a single-edged razor blade or a sharp knife to give the cleanest possible cut. Crushed stem cells and hanging strands of tissue cause problems you want to avoid. Remove side shoots, leaves, flowers, and flower buds from the lower half of the stem. Trim any large leaves, leaving between one-third and one-half of their surface.

2 Dip the lower one-third to one-half of the stem in rooting powder; this is a hormone stimulant that helps encourage root growth. Gently tap the stem to knock off excess powder.

3 Poke a hole in the rooting medium and insert a cutting to between one-third and one-half of its length. Firm the rooting medium around the stem with your fingers. When all the cuttings are inserted, water them in place.

4 A large, clear plastic bag forms a mini-greenhouse over the cuttings. Insert sticks or stakes around the container edge to hold the plastic away from the cuttings. Lift the edge of the plastic for an hour or so each day to allow air circulation. Water the rooting medium with lukewarm water as needed— this won't be often since the plastic cover helps retain moisture. To avoid rot, take care not to keep the cuttings continually soaking wet.

5 Gently lift out a cutting to check for roots. Some plants root more quickly than others: It may take from one week to one month for roots to show. When roots are ¼-inch long, use a spoon or fork as a small trowel for lifting out cuttings. Plant them in small 1½- to 2-inch pots filled with potting mix. Wait and replant them into larger pots or into the garden when a good strong root system has formed.

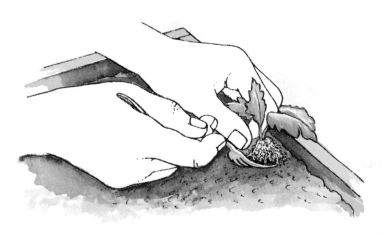

Planting Root Cuttings Vertically

Root cuttings are made from 1- to 3-inch sections of the parent plant's roots. When planting them vertically for rooting, be sure that the part that was nearest the main root is up and the part that was farther out is at the bottom. As you cut the root into sections, you can distinguish "up" from "down" by cutting the "up" side straight across and the "down" side on a slant. Plant so that the top of the cutting is ¼-inch above the surface of the medium—potting soil is a good rooting medium for root cuttings.

Division of Perennial Clumps by Hand

The simplest way to divide loosely woven perennial clumps is by pulling them apart with your hands, or by digging off a portion with a trowel or spade. Divide them into several large clumps rather than into many very small ones; this will provide fewer plants, but they'll be more vital and sure to produce flowers the first season after division.

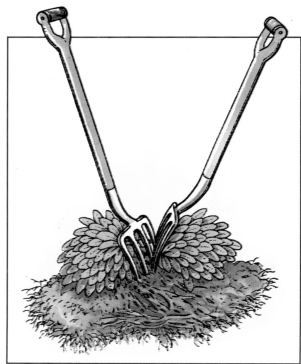

Using Spading Forks to Divide Perennial Clumps

When the perennial clump is more tightly bound together, two spading forks can be stuck through it back-to-back while it's still in the ground. By pushing out on the fork handles, it's usually possible to pry the clump apart. Some are so tenacious, however, that they must be hacked into chunks with a heavy knife, cleaver, or hatchet. Don't be afraid of doing the plant any harm—those that are this tough won't be fazed by such treatment!

Dividing Rhizomes

Some perennials have large, fleshy underground stems called rhizomes. Bearded irises are one example. To divide these types, dig up the entire clump and shake out the dirt. Then use a sharp knife to cleanly cut them into smaller clumps containing three or more buds. Let the pieces air dry for about an hour so the wounds can seal over before replanting them.

This beautifully landscaped perennials garden combines colorful blooms in various sizes and shapes with foliage of different textures and forms. The pond and garden sculpture contribute to the peaceful look.

LANDSCAPING WITH PERENNIALS

Because of the permanence of perennials, it pays to give advance consideration to where to plant them and which ones to use. You'll do some shifting and adjustment as you see the plantings develop, but you'll want to keep this to a minimum. It's certainly easier to make changes on paper!

Instead of buying the plants first, and then looking at your site for a place to put them, you should reverse the order. *First* study the site. Walk around the yard and take note of its special features: a steep bank, shaded areas, a wet low spot, or a sun-filled alcove. Jot down notes of areas you plan to landscape.

If you have difficulty envisioning how an area might look when planted, create a three-dimensional mock-up: poke sticks or pieces of leafy brush into the ground where you want bushes and trees, and mark out flower beds and patio areas with stakes linked together by twine. Sit in the patio area and look out at the make-believe landscape. Study it from wherever you'll view it. Move the markers around until they produce the best arrangement. Install a permanent label in each location.

In this chapter you'll find information on how to plan perennial plantings for various situations.

Putting a Garden on Paper

This well-planned perennials garden combines blazingstars, ribbon grass, lavender, daylilies, and shasta daisies.

Planning a perennial flower garden for a succession of bloom all season long is a fairly complex undertaking. There are so many details that must be considered: light and soil preferences, the size and height of plants, the color and form of blooms, foliage texture, and plant growth habit all are important. And then there are those plants that can be planted under and between others to give two seasons of bloom in the same space: spring bulbs under summer- and fall-blooming plants, and summer lilies under plants that flower in spring or fall.

Initially, the thought of laying out such a plan can be daunting, but, taken one step at a time, it becomes less overwhelming.

The first step is to make a list of your plant favorites. Research the characteristics of each plant on the list to learn what size they'll grow to, when they bloom, what colors they come in, what kind of soil and light they prefer, etc. This will help you to select the best plant from your list for each spot you've marked in the yard.

Sketch the layout on a piece of paper and note your choices. For flower beds, lay out detailed plans of exactly which plants will go where.

First, plan locations of the basic year-round perennials as we've done in our sample layout. Then take a piece of tracing paper and lay it over the basic planting plan. Mark those areas where bulbs can be interplanted and choose suitable varieties. Finally, make up "proof sheets," as we have done, identifying which portions of the garden will be colorful during each segment of the growing season. Check to see whether or not it's well balanced. If not, make switches and changes as necessary. Double check to be certain no tall plants are in front of shorter ones, that there are no colors that are likely to clash, and that no shade lovers have been placed in a sunny bed, or vice versa. Inevitably, there will be a need for a few changes and substitutions as your garden grows, but by carefully studying your advance plan you can at least avoid the obvious mistakes.

From these plans you can then determine how many plants you need of each kind. With this information, you're ready to make your purchases and do your planting.

How to Plan a Garden

1 Mark out the locations for each kind of plant you want in the border using a list of your favorites as a reference. Keep in mind that tall plants should be at the back and low ones in front, the colors and blooming seasons should be mixed throughout the garden for balance, and a mixture of foliage colors and textures will help add interest to areas not in blossom. Select plants suitable for the amount of light and moisture available.

Pink : P
Blue : B
White : W

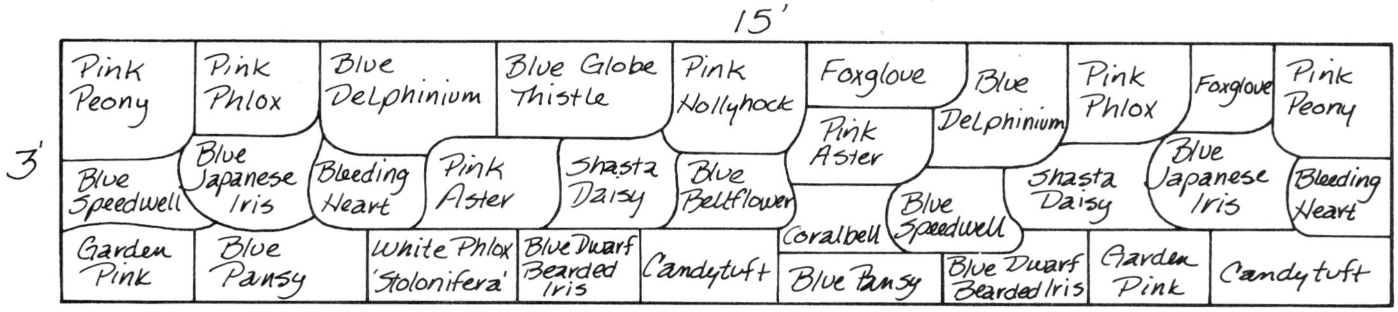

15'

| Pink Peony | Pink Phlox | Blue Delphinium | Blue Globe Thistle | Pink Hollyhock | Foxglove | Blue Delphinium | Pink Phlox | Foxglove | Pink Peony |

3'

Pink Aster

| Blue Speedwell | Blue Japanese Iris | Bleeding Heart | Pink Aster | Shasta Daisy | Blue Bellflower | | | Shasta Daisy | Blue Japanese Iris | Bleeding Heart |

Coralbell   Blue Speedwell

| Garden Pink | Blue Pansy | White Phlox 'Stolonifera' | Blue Dwarf Bearded Iris | Candytuft | Blue Pansy | Blue Dwarf Bearded Iris | Garden Pink | Candytuft |

Garden in Full Sun

Favorites —

Bleeding Heart	- P,W	Pansy	- B,W
Candytuft	- W	Peony	- B,W
Delphinium	- B,W	Phlox	- P
Foxglove	- B,W	Speedwell	- B
Japanese Iris	- B,W	Tulip	- P,B,W
Madonna Lily	- W		

2 Once all of the garden is laid out, place a sheet of tracing paper over the plan and mark those areas in which a double season of bloom is possible—by underplanting with spring flowering bulbs or summer flowering lilies, or by intermixing plants that die back early in the season with others that will expand and cover the same space after they're finished for the year.

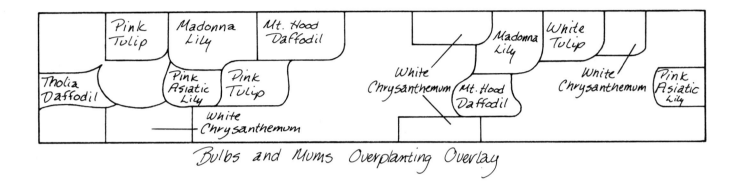

Bulbs and Mums Overplanting Overlay

3 Using the basic plan and the overlay as a guide, create a separate "proof" sheet on tracing paper for each portion of the flowering season: spring, early summer, late summer, and fall. Do this by marking each section of the garden that will be in flower and what colors they will be during that season. Study these to see what changes are needed to improve the balance of color through the entire growing season.

Pink = P
Blue : B
White : W

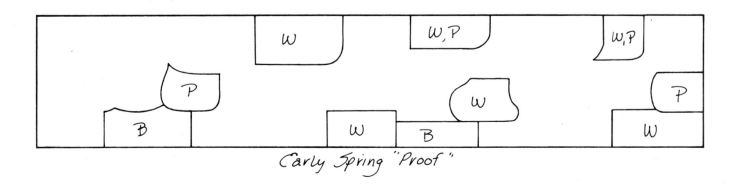

Early Spring "Proof"

Pink = P
Blue : B
White : W

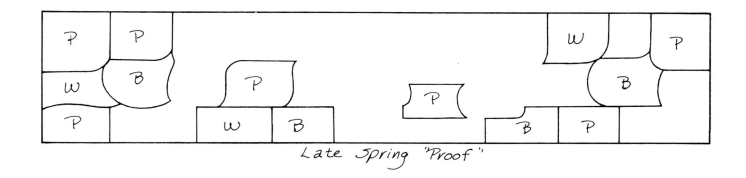

Late Spring "Proof"

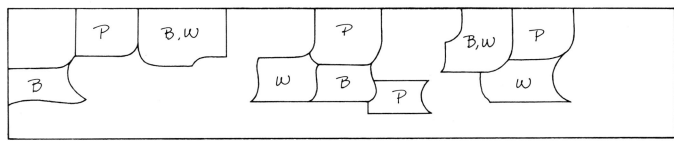

Early Summer "Proof"

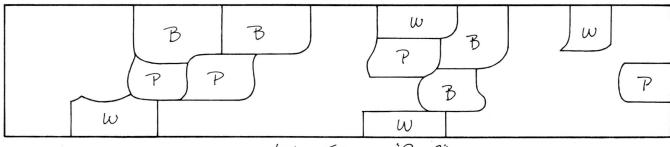

Late Summer "Proof"

Entrance Gardens, Borders, & Island Beds

A perennials border certainly adds beauty to this house.

The border layout we used as an example in the preceding section is a simple rectangular one suitable for use in front of a fence, hedge, side of a building, or row of flowering shrubs. But this is not the only setting and these are not the only proportions suitable for perennial plantings.

Nor do you have to exclusively use perennials in a planting. It's perfectly acceptable to mix annuals with perennials, and even—when the bed space is large enough to allow it—to include trees and evergreen or flowering shrubs in the design.

Because they're not demanding, perennials are ideally suited for use as often as possible in entrance gardens, as well as in borders and island beds.

The approach for laying out such plantings is similar to that shown for our side border, but there are some additional points that must be considered.

For example, the unique aspect of an entrance garden is that it will be viewed very briefly. This is an area people are likely to move through quickly rather than linger in or sit and view for an extended period. Therefore, it must be planted simply and for immediate impact. This is not the place for subtle combinations and rare species; it's where a bold, eye-catching display is needed.

This doesn't necessarily mean that it must be bright or garish; repeated or massed groups of white or pastel flowers can be effective, too. Even an all-foliage display can be dramatic when well chosen. Ornamental grasses, ferns, hostas, rosemary, stonecrops, bergenias, Japanese irises, wormwoods, and many others offer wonderful foliage colors and textures to work with.

Plants with strong perfumes are also more likely to be enjoyed in this situation where more subtle perfumes might go unnoticed. Sometimes these strong perfumes, which can be overpowering adjacent to an outdoor sitting area where they're constantly being inhaled, are ideal for short-term enjoyment.

In contrast to entrance gardens, flower plantings that will be enjoyed at leisure either while sitting among them outdoors or viewing them from inside, may be more low-key in their design. They should invite the eye to keep coming back for another look to perhaps discover additional aspects that weren't obvious at first. Here, of course, the plantings will be more interesting if there are contrasts of flowers, foliage textures, and colors.

Island beds—plantings that are centrally placed and viewed from all sides—require a somewhat different design approach than side beds. In order to be effective from every direction, it's necessary to lay them out so that the tallest plants are located in the middle of the bed rather than at the rear. It is therefore necessary to have many more plants of low and intermediate heights in these plantings than tall ones.

Flower beds come in all sizes and outlines; they can be shaped asymmetrically to fit any corner or contour desired. Squared off symmetrical beds have a rather formal appearance; curving meandering ones are more natural and informal looking. Choose a layout that best suits the surrounding garden, your house style, and your personal preferences.

Eye-Catching Entrance Garden

Entrance gardens should be simple in layout yet
eye-catching. Otherwise, they may not be noticed
during the brief moments they're viewed.

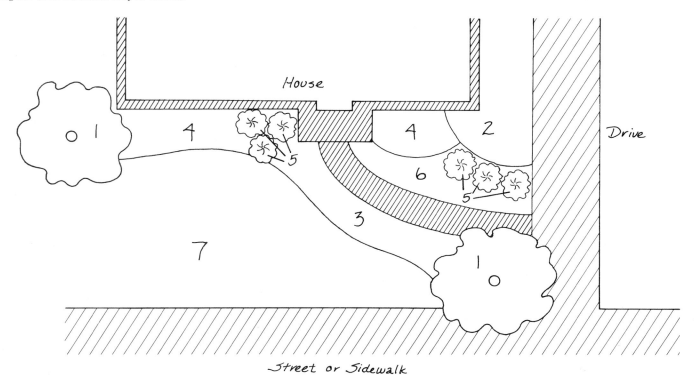

Note: The lists below are to be used for making a selection
of *one* variety for each area. Entries should be kept simple for
best results and greatest impact.

1 Attractive specimen shrub or small tree:
Golden Arborvitae (columnar variety)
Cutleaf Red Maple
Redbud
Silverbell

2 Broadleaf evergreens:
Boxwood
Ilex
Pieris
Rhododendron

3 Low, neat-growing perennials:
Candytuft
Hosta
Lavender
Lily Turf
Stonecrop

4 Medium-height perennials or flowering shrubs:
Azaleas
Daylilies
Peonies
Roses

5 Dramatic grass clumps:
Fountain Grass
Maiden Grass
Variegated Molinia

6 Second choice from group #3

7 Lawn

Corner Beds & Side Borders

Borders come in a wide variety of sizes and shapes. Their outline and plant content depends on the surrounding landscape, the land contours, and your own personal tastes.

= Tall plants

= Intermediate plants

= Low plants

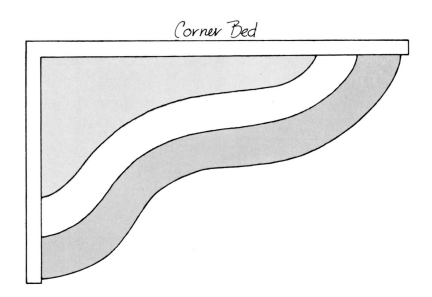

Corner Bed

Side Border

Wall, Fence, or Other Solid Background

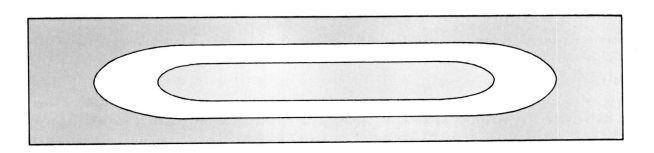

= Tall plants

= Intermediate plants

= Low plants

Island beds are surrounded on all sides by lawn or paving, so they are seen from every direction. It becomes a challenge to have them looking nice from all sides. Planning the layout of an island bed differs from a side border because the tallest flowers are clustered in the center of it, rather than arranged along the back edge.

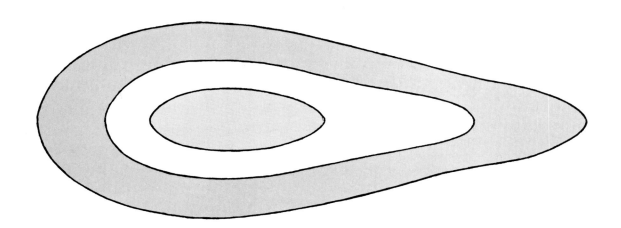

Perennials in Containers

Using garden troughs as containers for perennials planting is a novel idea.

I n most instances, perennials are best grown directly in the ground. However, there are occasions when it's desirable to grow them in containers as potted plants.

When the garden soil is so poor that it's nearly impossible to successfully grow plants in it, container plantings can be the solution. They can also be the answer for soil-less locations such as an apartment balcony, a deck, or a patio.

A third reason for raising container-grown perennials is to allow you to have those varieties that are not winter hardy in your climate. By growing them in containers, it's possible to easily move them into the house or a special shelter over the winter, then back into the garden in the spring.

Finally, it's sometimes nice to grow perennials as indoor plants, providing attractive displays within your home. After all, most houseplants are, in fact, perennials that are tropical and therefore not hardy for growing outdoors in most parts of the country. Some gardeners enjoy the novelty of growing various perennial bulbs in containers for winter bloom: tulips, daffodils, hyacinths, amaryllis, and lilies are popular choices.

Because of the extra care and space year-round container-grown plants require, you'll probably limit yourself to growing only those that are your special favorites—perennials that look beautiful both while they're in bloom and when they are not and those that add appreciably to the decor of your home and garden.

In order for plants to prosper in containers, a primary rule is that the pots must have adequate water drainage capability. Other major needs of potted plants are frequent watering, regular feeding, and repotting when they show signs of becoming rootbound. An easy way to check is by knocking the plant out of the pot every six months to see how jammed with roots it has become—when they're solidly matted, it's time to shift into a slightly larger pot, or to divide the plant into several pieces and repot.

To carry warm weather plants successfully through the winter in cold climates, it's necessary to bring them into the house or a greenhouse where warmth can be maintained. For those plants that are half-hardy or require only slightly milder winters than those you have, it's possible to place them on an unheated enclosed porch or other similar location where daylight sun can reach them, but they're not subjected to extremely low temperatures. If sub-zero temperatures persist, a small space heater on a low setting will provide enough heat to prevent damage. Don't make it so warm that tender new growth is encouraged to sprout—just fend off the very coldest conditions for the brief periods that they last.

Remember that potted plants overwintered under these conditions will require periodic watering in order to keep them from drying out. Such waterings should be infrequent as the plant's metabolism is much slower in cold conditions.

GOOD PLANT CHOICES TO GROW IN CONTAINERS

Asparagus Fern	Ferns
Rex Begonia*	Geranium
Bleeding Heart	Kalanchoe*
Chrysanthemum	Lavender
Clivia*	African Lily
Yellow Coneflower	Big Blue Lily Turf
Daylily	Purple Loosestrife
Espalier and Tree	Rose Mallow
Forms of	Marguerite*
Chrysanthemum,	Oxalis*
Fuchsia, Geranium,	Poinsettia*
Lantana*, and	Russian Sage
Rose Mallow	Stonecrop

* = Not winter hardy

Gardening in Containers

This cross-section drawing shows the best way to plant in a container. To grow plants successfully in containers, good drainage is essential. Drainage holes need to be covered to keep in soil: Pieces of broken pottery, fine screening, or a coffee filter may be used. If additional drainage is needed, add a layer of small stones, perlite, or coarse sand in the bottom of the container. If the container is located where dripping water would do damage, place a drip tray under the container to catch excess water.

Using Decorative Containers

When using a decorative container that has no drainage holes, place a well-drained pot inside of it and actually grow the plants in this inner pot. Raise the inner pot on a layer of pebbles to keep it above water level. The space between the inner and outer pots can be filled with peat moss to provide insulation that helps stabilize soil temperatures.

How to Care for Container-Grown Plants

Perennials in containers must receive special care over winter in cold climates. Keep them in the house or a greenhouse if they are tropical varieties. Those that withstand freezing can be kept in an unheated area such as an enclosed porch and will only require some heating during prolonged, extreme cold spells. Watering should be cut back severely during this dormant period.

A unique planting of perennials adds beauty to an entrance gate. These lovely purple Siberian irises certainly draw attention to themselves. Their intense color is softened by the white daisies behind them and by the profusion of foliage around them.

CHAPTER 6

ENCYCLOPEDIA OF PERENNIAL FAVORITES

Perennials are certainly versatile plants. They can grow in good soil and poor soil; some flourish in full sun, and others are quite content with deep shade. The sizes and shapes nature provides them with are so diverse that any gardener can select perennials to suit his or her garden location and conditions.

The following encyclopedia was designed in order to help gardeners in all regions of the United States make the best perennial selections possible. Botanical and common names, descriptions, ease of care, how-to-grow techniques, propagation, uses, and related species and varieties are all dealt with in depth. Color bars identifying zones that each specimen is congenial to are provided. For example, if a perennial is listed under Zone 5, this means that Zone 5 is the coldest zone at which the plant is hardy. Photos are included for each entry.

The adaptability of perennials truly makes them all-purpose plants. Whether you want to design a garden strictly with perennials, add color to an annuals garden in certain seasons, create a unique rock garden, or try your hand at a wet garden, you will find plants here that will work for you. And if you like what you created, you have the satisfaction of knowing that with a little bit of work your garden can flourish year after year.

Hardy Ageratum, Mist Flower

Eupatorium coelestinum
Zone: USDA 6

The fuzzy, blue flowers of this plant resemble those of the annual bedding ageratum or floss flower. The genus is named for King Eupator of Pontis, who discovered one species was an antidote to a poison.

Description: Hardy ageratums are 2-foot mounds of triangular, coarsely-toothed leaves and flat-topped flower clusters that bloom early in the fall.

Ease of care: Easy.

How to grow: Eupatoriums prefer a good, well-drained but moist garden soil in full sun or partial shade. They like a bit of shade in places with hot summers. Plants appear late in the spring; digging them up by mistake should be avoided.

Propagation: By division in early spring or by seed.

Uses: The showy blue flowers are welcome in early fall and the plants are excellent in a border or used as edging.

Related species: Both *Eupatorium maculatum* and *E. purpureum* are handsome American wildflowers called joe-pye weed. *E. maculatum* grows to 6 feet tall and bears rounded heads of many small, thinly fringed, purple to light purple flowers on stems that are shaded or spotted purple. *E. purpureum* has stems that are usually green, and the flowers smell of vanilla. Both are spectacular in the back of a border. Although adaptable to average garden soil, they prefer an evenly moist spot.

Japanese Anemone

Anemone species
Zone: USDA 5b

The genus comes from the Greek word for "wind," and many of the plants in this family are called wind flowers. They are listed as *Anemone* x *hybrida*.

Description: The strong-stemmed and showy flowers have 5 or more petal-like sepals that enclose numerous golden stamens with compound and very attractive leaves. Mature clumps can reach a height of 5 feet.

Ease of care: Easy.

How to grow: These plants are not difficult to grow but do need a fertile, moist soil with plenty of organic matter mixed in as the roots (or rhizomes) resent heavy clay and wet earth and will rot in those conditions. Anemones enjoy full sun in northern gardens but will easily adjust to partial shade. In southern gardens, they need partial shade. In areas that have severe winters with little snow cover, plants should be mulched in late fall. In colder areas of the country, many flowers are destroyed by early frosts, so they must be protected.

Propagation: By division in early spring or by root division.

Uses: Anemones are especially beautiful when grown in large clumps.

Related varieties: A number of varieties are found, including 'Alba,' with white flowers; 'Mont Rose,' with deep rose flowers; and 'Queen Charlotte,' bearing semi-double, pink flowers. *Anemone vitifolia* is similar, but the pink-blossomed plants are hardier and more tolerant both of sun and of drier soil. It is usually sold as 'Robustissima' and blooms a month earlier than *Anemone* x *hybrida*.

Golden Aster

Chrysopsis mariana
Zone: USDA 5

This is an American native flower spreading from eastern New York to Ohio and then south to Texas and Florida. The genus name means "golden aspect" and refers to the color of the flowers.

Description: Silky stems, often with a purplish stain, grow to 3 feet in height with leaves that are woolly when young, becoming smooth with age. The leaves have a pronounced midrib. Flower sprays are bright yellow, blooming in late summer and on into fall.

Ease of care: Easy.

How to grow: Golden asters like full sun or just a bit of shade, doing well in hot weather with average garden soil. This is a good drought-resistant plant found growing in sandy soil in the wild.

Propagation: By division or by seed.

Uses: The golden aster is fine for the wild garden or planted in borders. It makes a fine addition to the autumn garden, where it will mix well with other asters. Seeds sown in early spring will produce flowering plants the first year.

Stoke's Aster

Stokesia laevis
Zone: USDA 5b

Stoke's aster is a native American wildflower that resembles a China aster, originally found from South Carolina to Florida and Louisiana. It is surprisingly hardy as far north as Rochester, New York. It is named in honor of Dr. Jonathan Stokes, an English botanist.

Description: Leaves are alternate, spiny-toothed toward the base, with the upper leaves clasping the stem. Fluffy blue to lavender flowers are 2 to 5 inches across on well-branched, 1- to 2-foot stems.

Ease of care: Easy.

How to grow: Stokesias need full sun and a good, well-drained soil. New plants take a year or two to settle in before maximum bloom. They should be mulched in areas with bad winters and little snow cover. Remove spent blooms for flowers to continue blooming until September.

Propagation: By seed or by division in spring.

Uses: Stokesias are very decorative flowers for the front of the bed or border. Plants can also be forced for winter bloom in the greenhouse. They are good cut flowers, and the seedpods are excellent in dried arrangements.

Related varieties: 'Alba' is the pure white form; 'Blue Danube' is blue; and 'Silver Moon' is icy white.

Astilbe, Garden Spiraea

Astilbe species
Zone: USDA 5

Beautiful plants for the garden, the astilbes available to gardeners today are usually the result of hybridizing and listed as *Astilbe* x *Arendsii* in garden books and nursery catalogs. The botanical name means "without brilliance" and refers to the lack of punch in the individual flowers.

Description: Astilbes are lovely plants both for their dark green, fernlike foliage growing on polished stems and their long panicles (or spikes) of flowers that resemble feathery plumes. Individual blossoms are small, but as each head contains dozens of branches and each branch bears hundreds of flowers, the total effect is one of beauty. Depending on the type, they can bloom from midsummer to the end of August.

Ease of care: Easy.

How to grow: Astilbes do well in full sun but are best with partial shade, especially in the southern parts of the country. Soil should be good and moist with plenty of organic matter mixed in. Divide the clumps every third year.

Propagation: By division.

Uses: The larger varieties work well in the garden border as specimen plants, even though most of them should be set out in groups of three or more. Colors include white, pink, red, rose, and lilac. Heights vary from 12 to 40 inches. The white forms are especially effective against a shrub border or a line of bushes. They also make an effective ground cover. Astilbes turn a lovely shade of brown in the fall, with the dried flower heads persisting until beaten down by heavy snow. They can be used as cut flowers in the summer and then dried for winter floral arrangements. Finally, astilbes can be forced for winter flowering by potting them in the fall, rooting them, and bringing them into greenhouse heat with plenty of water.

Related species: *Astilbe chinensis* 'Pumila' originally came from China and Japan. The flowers are a mauve-pink on 8- to 12-inch stems, perfect along the edge of a border and in the rock garden as they can tolerate a drier soil than others. *Astilbe tacquetii* 'Superba' is also from China and bears large plumes of rose-pink flowers resembling cotton candy on 4-foot stems.

Related varieties: 'Bridal Veil' bears white flowers on 2-foot stems; 'Peach Blossom' has salmon-pink flowers on 26-inch stems; pink 'Erica' is on 30-inch stems; and 'Montgomery' is a clear red on 28-inch stems.

Avens

Geum species
Zone: **USDA 6**

The avens are members of the rose family. They produce brilliant flowers and plants with attractive leaves coated with silky down. *Geum* is the original Latin name for the herb Bennet (*Geum urbanum*), a plant with an astringent root once used in medicine. Most of the garden forms are hybrids of two or more species.

Description: Avens have clumps of attractive, lobed, shiny green leaves covered with silky down on hairy stems. The plants grow to 2 feet tall and bear single flowers about 1½ inches across. Flower colors are red, yellow, or white. They bloom in spring and summer.

Ease of care: Easy.

How to grow: Avens are plants for cool summers. They prefer full sun and a well-drained but moist soil with plenty of humus. The plants should be divided every two years. In areas subject to below zero temperatures without snow cover, these plants should be mulched.

Propagation: By division in spring or by seed.

Uses: Avens are attractive in the front of a border and in a rock garden where the bright flowers are very showy.

Related varieties: 'Mrs. Bradshaw' is a double, brilliant scarlet and 'Lady Stratheden' is a warm yellow.

Baby's Breath

Gypsophila paniculata
Zone: **USDA 5**

Almost everyone has given or received a bouquet of flowers from the florist that contained a few sprays of baby's breath. The genus is Latin for the phrase "friendship with gypsum," because one species, *Gypsophila repens,* has been found growing on gypsum rocks.

Description: Small, blue-green leaves, almost fleshy, on stems with slightly swollen joints bear a profusion of many-branched panicles containing numerous ⅛-inch wide flowers. Plants bloom in June and July.

Ease of care: Easy.

How to grow: Baby's breath require full sun and a good, deep, well-drained garden soil with humus. Even though the plants have tap roots, they still require liberal amounts of water. If the soil is at all acid, a cup of ground limestone per square yard should be added into the soil surrounding these lime-loving plants. Tall plants will probably require staking. They will rebloom if spent flowers are removed.

Propagation: By seed. Propagation by cuttings requires patience, skill, and luck.

Uses: Baby's breath are wonderful for filling in gaps in a bed or border. They are especially lovely when tumbling over rock walls or falling out of a raised bed.

Related species: *Gypsophila repens* is a creeping baby's breath that grows 6 inches high, but covers an area to a width of 3 feet. 'Alba' is white; 'Rosea' is pink.

Related varieties: Two popular varieties are 'Bristol Fairy,' with pure white, double flowers, that grows to a height of 4 feet, and 'Pink Fairy,' reaching 18 inches in height with pink doubles.

Balloon Flower

Platycodon grandiflorus
Zone: **USDA 4**

A one-species genus, balloon flowers are so named because the unopened flowers look like small and rounded hot-air blimps. They are originally from Japan. The genus is named for the Greek word for "broad bell" and refers to the flower shape.

Description: Balloon flowers are clump-forming perennials with alternate leaves of a light green on stems usually between 1½ and 3 feet tall. They bear balloon-shaped buds that open to bell-shaped flowers with 5 points and are 2 to 3 inches wide. The sap is milky.

Ease of care: Easy.

How to grow: Balloon flowers like moist, well-drained soil in full sun or partial shade. They prefer places with cool summers. Plan the plant's position carefully as it is not until late spring that the first signs of life appear.

Propagation: By division in mid-spring or by seed.

Uses: Blooming for most of the summer, balloon flowers are attractive in borders, with the smaller types growing best along garden edges. They are especially effective when used in conjunction with white pansies or the white obedient plant.

Related varieties: 'Album' bears white flowers, and 'Hakona Blue' has two layers of petals, both on 16-inch stems. 'Mariesii' has blue flowers on 12- to 16-inch stems, and 'Shell Pink' bears larger flowers of a soft-pink on 2-foot stems and is best in some shade.

Basket-of-Gold, Goldentuft, Madwort

Aurinia saxatilis
Zone: USDA 5

Originally included in the *Alyssum* genus, these charming flowers of spring have now been moved to an older genus named after a chemical dyestuff used to stain paper. They belong to the mustard family.

Description: Attractive and low gray foliage growing in dense mats gives rise to clusters of golden-yellow, 4-petaled flowers floating 6 to 12 inches above the plants.

Ease of care: Easy.

How to grow: Aurinias need only well-drained, average soil in full sun. Plants will easily rot in damp locations and resent high humidity. They can be sheared after blooming.

Propagation: By cuttings or by seed.

Uses: Aurinias are quite happy growing in the spaces between stone walks, carpeting the rock garden, or growing in pockets in stone walls where their flowers become tumbling falls of gold.

Related varieties: *Alyssum montanum*, 'Mountain Gold,' 4 inches tall, with silvery, evergreen leaves and fragrant, bright yellow flowers makes a dense ground cover. 'Citrina' bears lemon-yellow flowers; 'Flore Plena' has double, yellow blooms; and 'Compacta' has a denser habit of growth.

Beard Tongue

Penstemon barbatus
Zone: USDA 4

There are so many kinds of penstemons that the American Penstemon Society publishes a newsletter and illustrated guides for choosing these plants. Except for one species from Asia, all the rest are native to North America, with most coming from the West Coast. The genus name refers to the presence of a fifth stamen.

Description: Basal foliage is evergreen in warmer climates. The leaves are sometimes whorled. Flowers are tubular in airy, terminal clusters atop strong stems, blooming from spring into summer.

Ease of care: Moderately easy.

How to grow: Penstemons come from areas with rough growing conditions and should never be exposed to wet or damp earth. A thin, rocky soil in full sun is best. Of all the species, *P. barbatus* seems to do the best in the East.

Propagation: By division in spring or by seed.

Uses: Penstemons are exceedingly attractive in the garden and have a long season of bloom. Plants are best set out in groups so that a mass of flowers is in view. For those who succumb to their beauty, entire specialty gardens can be made of only this genus. They are excellent as cut flowers.

Related varieties: 'Alba' has white flowers; 'Elfin Pink' has clear pink flowers on 1-foot high branches, making it perfect for the front of the border; 'Prairie Fire' is a vivid orange-red on 22-inch stems; and 'Prairie Dusk' has purple flowers on 20-inch stems.

Bellflower

Campanula species
Zone: USDA 4

The botanical name is from the Latin word for "bell" and refers to the shape of the flowers. The genus includes annual flowers, biennials, and perennials suitable for the formal garden and the wild garden. *Campanula rapunculoides* is a wild weed and should be avoided. *C. rapunculus* can be considered for the vegetable garden, since the rampion has roots that are used in salads.

Description: Bellflowers are usually in various shades of blue, and many are available in white. Flowers bloom from late spring into early summer. Basal leaves are usually broader than the stem leaves and form rosettes or mats.

Ease of care: Easy.

How to grow: Bellflowers need a good, moist, but well-drained soil with plenty of organic matter mixed in. In the North, plants will tolerate full sun as long as the soil is not dry, but elsewhere a spot in semi-shade is preferred.

Propagation: By division or by seed.

Uses: According to the species, plants are beautiful in the border, useful in the rock garden, and fine for the shade or wild garden. Many species, including *Campanula isophylla*, the star-of-Bethlehem, also do well when grown in pots.

Related species: *Campanula carpatica* is from the Carpathian mountains of Europe, blooming at a height of 10 inches with solitary blue flowers. It is effective as an edging or tumbling over a small rock cliff. Among the many varieties: a white form called 'Alba' as well as 'Blue Carpet,' a smaller, more compact form. *Campanula Elatines* var *garganica*,

(continued)

Delphinium, Larkspur

Delphinium species
Zone: USDA 4 to 6

The genus of this plant comes from the Greek word for "dolphin" and is suggested by the shape of a gland in the blossoms that secretes nectar. Many delphiniums are poisonous to cattle.

Description: The alternate leaves are cut and divided. Plants produce tall spikes of showy flowers, usually in shades of blue, each having a long spur behind the petals.

Ease of care: Moderately difficult.

How to grow: Delphiniums are worth almost any effort to grow because they are so beautiful. They need full sun and a good, deep, well-drained, evenly moist soil that has a high humus content. If the soil is too acid, agricultural lime should be added. They are hardy feeders that must be supplied with compost or well-rotted manure, benefiting from feedings of a 5-10-5 fertilizer every year. The area where they grow should have some protection from high winds because the hollow flower stalks, though strong, are often so covered with flowers that they can easily break in the breeze. Many gardens use delphiniums in front of stone walls for this reason. Without such protection, the gardener will have to resort to staking. After flowering, flower heads should be removed unless seeds are wanted. Surprisingly, these plants are very cold-hardy and resent hot climates and long, blistering summers. Delphiniums are short-lived perennials that lose their vitality after two to three years. Since they grow easily from seeds and cuttings, propagation is never a problem.

Propagation: By cuttings, by seed, or by careful division.

Uses: Short delphiniums can be used in the front of a garden, the Belladonna hybrids in the middle, and the tall Pacific Coast hybrids in the rear. They are excellent cut flowers, too.

Related species: Only hardy to USDA 8, *Delphinium cardinale*, or scarlet larkspurs, are lovely flowers for the summer garden. *Delphinium elatum*, or the candle larkspur, is one of the sources for many of the most beautiful delphinium hybrids today. Reaching to 6 feet, the flowers are now available in white, lavender, blue, and purple. The Belladonna hybrids are light blue with 5-foot stalks and, if spent flowers are removed, they will usually produce blooms all summer long. 'Casa Blanca' is pure white. The Blackmore and Langdon hybrids were first developed in 1905. Today's plants bear pastel blue, lavender, white, violet, and indigo flowers on 4- to 5-foot stems. The Pacific Coast hybrids produce 7-foot stalks that must be staked even when given protection; the flowers in various shades of blue and pink are spectacular. 'Magic Fountain' is a dwarf version growing to 30 inches with double blooms. 'Connecticut Yankee' is a bush delphinium with single flowers of mixed colors on 30-inch stalks. *Delphinium grandiflorum* (sometimes called *D. chinensis*), or the Siberian larkspur, has finely cut foliage and blue flowers on 2- to 3-foot stalks, blooming the first year from seed if started early. 'Blue Mirror' has gentian-blue flowers, and 'Alba' is white.

Edelweiss

Leontopodium alpinum
Zone: USDA 5

Edelweiss means "noble white" in German. This is the plant that supposedly has led to the death of stalwart youths who, when reaching from mountain crags for the blooms, missed their footing and fell into the abyss. The genus name means "lion's foot" and refers to the shape and woolly aspect of the flower.

Description: Tufted plants with gray and woolly leaves grow to about 12 inches in height. Small flower heads are surrounded by starlike clusters of white, woolly bracts.

Ease of care: Easy.

How to grow: Edelweiss want full sun, well-drained sandy or gritty soil, and will not survive wet soil in the winter. In areas without snow cover, protect the plants from rain and sleet with glass.

Propagation: By seed sown in spring.

Uses: Edelweiss are perfect for the rock garden, as the woolly plants look best when used in conjunction with stone.

Pearly Everlasting

Anaphalis species
Zone: USDA 4a

Pearly everlastings bear the genus name of *Anaphalis,* said to be an ancient Greek name for a similar plant. They are members of the daisy family. Their common name refers to their everlasting quality when dried, and many a farmer's mantlepiece held winter bouquets using this American wildflower.

Description: The American species, *Anaphalis margaritacea,* grows as a wildflower over much of the country. It is 2 feet tall and has slender, pointed leaves that are green on top and gray underneath. Small clusters of ¼-inch white flowers bloom in the summer. *Anaphalis triplinervis* comes from the alpine Himalayas. It has silvery gray leaves in the spring that turn green as summer progresses. Flowers bloom in clusters from midsummer until frost.

Ease of care: Easy.

How to grow: Both species are easy to grow, adapting to most soil conditions, but *Anaphalis triplinervis* is not as rangy as *A. margaritacea* and better for the perennial border. It will also adapt to a moist soil. Plants grow up to 18 inches in height bearing 6-inch leaves of a silvery gray color. *Anaphalis margaritacea* will grow to 20 inches and is especially valuable in dry situations as it will survive and bloom on dry hillsides. It is also a welcome addition to the wild garden.

Propagation: By division in spring or fall or by seed.

Uses: The gray leaf color adds a welcome change from the greens found in the typical summer garden. In late summer, the plants begin to bloom and bear many clusters of small, white blossoms with petals—really bracts—that feel and look like shiny paper. They are easy to dry for winter bouquets. After autumn winds blow away the seeds, only the attractive outer bracts are left.

Fleabane

Erigeron hybridus
Zone: USDA 5

Fleabanes are members of the daisy family that closely resemble asters. Their common name is a salute to the belief that they once controlled the ravages of fleas. The genus name is from the Greek and means "an early old man," probably referring to the early flowering and fruiting of some species.

Description: Fleabanes have narrow leaves that are smooth above and woolly underneath. The flowers are densely fringed in clusters on 18-inch stems.

Ease of care: Easy.

How to grow: Fleabanes prefer good, well-drained garden soil in full sun. They prefer slight shade in areas of hot summers.

Propagation: By division in early spring, by cuttings, or by seed.

Uses: Fleabanes are excellent in the rock garden, the formal bed or border, and the wild garden. Plant them in drifts as the flowers look best when more than one plant is used. They are excellent as cut flowers.

Related species: *Erigeron speciosus* 'Azure Fairy' has semi-double, lavender flowers on 30-inch stems.

Related varieties: 'Foerster's Liebling' has double, pink flowers; 'Double Beauty' bears double, violet-blue flowers; and 'Prosperity' has semi-double, mauve-blue flowers.

Chinese Forget-Me-Not

Cynoglossum nervosum
Zone: USDA 5

Cynoglossum, the Greek word for "hound's tongue," and "Chinese forget-me-not" are both aptly chosen names. The delightful flowers resemble the common garden forget-me-not (*Myosotis sylvatica*), and the leaves indeed look like Fido with an open mouth.

Description: Large, hairy, rough leaves grow on stems up to 30 inches high. They are topped with many sprays of ³/₅-inch, gentian-blue flowers that bloom in July, lasting well into August.

Ease of care: Easy.

How to grow: Cynoglossums want full sun and a good, well-drained but moist soil. They will also do surprisingly well in dry soils. In good soil, growth will be exuberant and stems will flop over.

Propagation: By division in spring or by seed.

Uses: While the flowers are welcome in the formal garden bed or border, these plants seem better suited for the wild garden as the leaves can be quite unruly. Stems should be cut off in the fall.

Related variety: 'Dwarf Firmament' produces sky blue blossoms on 18-inch plants.

Yellow Foxglove

Digitalis grandiflora
Zone: USDA 4

Most foxgloves are biennial plants, but *Digitalis grandiflora* (still called *D. ambigua* in some catalogs) is a true perennial for the garden. The genus is named for the Latin word for "finger" in reference to the shape of the flower. The common name alludes to the belief that a fox could become invisible and make off with the chickens if it wore blossoms on its paws.

Description: Yellow foxgloves are strong-stemmed plants with simple alternate leaves. Their nodding bell-like flowers usually line up on one side of the stem and bloom in summer.

Ease of care: Easy.

How to grow: Yellow foxgloves want a good, moist, well-drained garden soil in partial shade. If dead flower stalks are removed, plants sometimes bloom a second time.

Propagation: By division or by seed.

Uses: Foxgloves are superb in the wild garden and among plants that have naturalized along the edge of a wooded area. They are also lovely in front of a line of shrubbery or small trees.

Related species: *Digitalis lutea* is a perennial from 2 to 3 feet high that bears many small, creamy yellow fingers on one side of each blooming stalk, flowering in May and June.

Gas Plant, Burning Bush

Dictamnus albus
Zone: USDA 4

There is only one species in this genus, and rumor has it that its leaves, if lighted with a match on a breathless summer evening, will produce a gas and burn with a faint glow. Many have tried, but few have reported success. The genus is named in honor of plants that grew on Mount Dicte in Crete.

Description: A handsome plant resembling a small bush, gas plants grow between 2 and 3 feet high with glossy, compound leaves and attractive white flowers. The leaves have a faint, lemony scent.

Ease of care: Easy.

How to grow: The location of a gas plant must be chosen with care. Once planted it will persist for decades, although it cannot be moved as its roots resent any disturbance. A spot in full sun with good, humus-rich, moist, and well-drained soil is needed. Plants are usually purchased as 2-year-old seedlings. Allow 3 feet between plants if grouped.

Propagation: By seed.

Uses: In flower or out, this is an attractive plant for the border since, even after flowering has passed, the seed heads provide visual interest.

Related varieties: 'Purpureus' bears pink flowers, and 'Rubra' has flowers of a rosy-purple.

Gaura

Gaura Lindheimeri
Zone: USDA 6

There are a number of gauras that are native American wildflowers; however, this particular species is the best for the garden. Found naturally from Louisiana to Texas and south to Mexico, the white flowers slowly fade to pink as they age. The genus is a Greek word for "proud," since many of the species are showy when in bloom.

Description: Gaura has alternate, lance-shaped leaves up to 3 inches long on stout stems. It blooms with 1-inch, white, 4-petaled flowers that age to pink and persist throughout the summer. Stems can reach to 6 feet.

Ease of care: Easy.

How to grow: Gauras need full sun in good, deep, well-drained garden soil as the tap root is very long. They are both drought- and heat-resistant.

Propagation: By division in spring or by seed.

Uses: Perfect for both a dry garden and a wild garden, they are also very attractive in a formal border. In northern climates, they bloom late in the season and are charming when planted with asters and ornamental grasses.

Globeflower

Trollius x *cultorum*
Zone: USDA 5

Globeflowers resemble large, double butter-cups or florist's ranunculus, with blossoms sitting like golden-yellow balls atop 30-inch stems. The genus name is from the Hungarian, *torolya*, a native name for the flower.

Description: Thick rootstocks slowly form large clumps that produce many strong stems with coarsely toothed leaves and one showy 2-inch flower per stem. Each flower has many waxy, rounded sepals and 5 or more petals, blooming in late May and June.

Ease of care: Easy.

How to grow: Globeflowers need a good, moist garden soil with plenty of humus. In the North, full sun will do as long as the soil is moist. They are better in partial shade. Remove spent flowers to promote further bloom.

Propagation: By division in fall or by seed.

Uses: Globeflowers are beautiful when planted in masses—both in sunny or shady borders. They are excellent waterside plants, doing well where others might not succeed. They make good cut flowers.

Related species: *Trollius europaeus* forms a compact clump and bears clear yellow flowers on 24-inch stems, blooming in late April and May. 'Superbus' is usually offered.

Related varieties: 'Byrne's Giant' is pure yellow, and 'Etna' is a dark orange—both are on 24-inch stems; 'Lemon Queen' is lemon-yellow on 28-inch stems; 'Orange Nassau' has orange flowers, and 'Prichard's Giant' bears large, deep golden-yellow flowers. It is one of the first to flower.

Goat's Beard, Wild Spirea

Aruncus dioicus
Zone: USDA 4

Goat's beard has been revered for years; the genus was named by Pliny, the Roman naturalist.

Description: Plants can grow as high as 6 feet and look like a bush. Then in early autumn, the plants come into bloom, producing many showy plumes of tiny, white flowers. The plants bring color to the garden after the usual spring show has passed.

Ease of care: Easy.

How to grow: Goat's beard is easy to grow as long as the gardener provides light shade and a moist soil. The plants are *dioecious,* meaning that male and female flowers grow on separate plants, but there is little difference between them, and most nurseries never mark the distinction. Goat's beard does very well in moist bottomland and should never lack for water in the summer.

Propagation: By division in the spring (difficult with older plants) or by seed.

Uses: Because it wants light shade rather than deep shadow, goat's beard is a fine choice for areas under groups of high trees. A waterside planting is also a good choice, especially when the plants have a background of trees.

Related species: *Aruncus aethusifolius* is a dwarf variety from Korea that makes a 6- to 8-inch mound of feathery leaves and 1-foot spires of white, plumelike blossoms, making an excellent edging for the garden border.

Related varieties: 'Kneiffi' is the cut-leaf goat's beard, reaching a height of 4 feet with leaves that are cut into narrow segments. 'Zweiweltenkind' bears white plumes of flowers on 4-foot plants.

Goldenrod

Solidago hybrids
Zone: USDA 5

Glorious flowers of the American fall, gold-enrods have suffered from bad press due to the mistaken belief that they cause hay fever and the fact that a few can become weedy when brought into the garden. Since most of the 130 or so species found in the wild cross-pollinate with ease, the plants described are unspecified hybrids. The genus name is from the Latin *solidare,* "to join," and refers to reputed healing properties.

Description: Goldenrods are strong-stemmed plants, often growing to 6 feet tall, with either smooth or lightly toothed alternate leaves arising from a root crown or rhizome. They bloom in late summer or fall with sprays of small, usually golden-yellow flowers.

Ease of care: Easy.

How to grow: Goldenrods are happy in full sun or partial shade with good, well-drained garden soil. They will also do well in moist conditions.

Propagation: By division in spring or by seed.

Uses: Great for the wild garden, stream side, or naturalized in meadow gardens, goldenrods are striking in the open bed or border. They are excellent for cutting.

Related varieties: 'Golden Mosa' has golden-yellow flowers on 2- to 3-foot stems. 'Cloth of Gold' has golden-yellow flowers, while 'Crown of Rays' bears yellow flowers—both are on 18-inch stems. 'Laurin' bears bright yellow flowers on 16-inch stems, and 'Golden Dwarf' has bright yellow blossoms on 1-foot stems.

Goldenstar

Chrysogonum virginianum
Zone: USDA 6

From Pennsylvania and West Virginia, then south to Florida and Louisiana, the goldenstar is an American native and the only species in this genus. The genus name means "golden joint" and refers to the blossoms rising from stem nodes.

Description: Yellow daisies about 2 inches across nod above hairy leaves on stems that creep and make a mound about 10 inches high, blooming from spring into summer. The leaves are evergreen and not particularly attractive.

Ease of care: Easy.

How to grow: If trying to grow this plant in the North, a sunny spot with protection from winter winds must be chosen. Lack of snow cover in Zone 5 will usually do it in. Well-drained, humus-rich soil is best and, while it does well in full sun, partial shade is best. When the plants first bloom, they are only a few inches high, but the last flowers of the season might be on stems 12 inches high. Nursery-grown specimens are often shorter than those from the wild.

Propagation: By seed or by division (only in the spring).

Uses: A star in the wild garden, a goldenstar is also an excellent ground cover and perfect for the rock garden.

Related varieties: Both 'Mark Viette' and 'Australis' are long-blooming clump forms. 'Allen Bush' is a rapid-spreading form that blooms heavily in the spring.

Goutweed, Ground Elder

Aegopodium Podagraria
Zone: USDA 3b

English gardeners can talk for hours about the evils of ground elder, or goutweed as it is called in the United States. The botanical name means "little goat feet," and the plants have the tenacity of that animal and can run through the garden, out of control, using roots that ramble as though they did have little feet.

Description: 'Variegatum' is a plant with very attractive leaves of light green that are edged with white. Plants grow about 1 foot high. The flowers are white, rangy, not very attractive, and should be cut off to prevent self-seeding.

Ease of care: Easy.

How to grow: Goutweed is almost too easy to grow, adapting to just about any garden soil. Plants like full sun, but will grow in partial or even full shade, making this a good choice for an edging along the north side of a house or in the open shade of a wooded area.

Propagation: By division in spring or fall.

Uses: This plant makes a fine ground cover or planting for a slope that is too steep either for grass or for a regular garden. If leaves turn brown from summer heat, they can be cut back and new fresh leaves will appear. Since each piece of root will eventually lead to a new plant, care should be taken in planting, especially if used in a formal garden. Plants should be grown in sunken tubs or in a strip between a shrub or tree background and a sidewalk or other solid edging. Goutweed also does well in containers.

Ornamental Grasses

Gramineae **family**
Zone: USDA 5

Ornamental grasses are a distinct family of plants unexcelled for the perennial garden. They are popular in English and European gardens. The grasses have no need for petals because they are fertilized by pollen grains that are carried from plant to plant by the wind. Still, grass flowers possess all the necessary sexual parts to produce seeds, and many of the seed heads of the grasses are very beautiful and have long been popular.

Description: The grass family (*Gramineae*) runs the gamut—from 120-foot giant bamboos (*Dendrocalamus giganteus*) to the tiny, dwarf fescues (*Festuca* spp.) only a few inches high. The stems, or culms, of the true grasses are usually round and hollow (although corn is solid), and the stem sections are joined by solid joints, or nodes. Root systems are very fibrous, growing deep into the ground, making them excellent plants in dry summers and invaluable for holding soil together. The leaves are always parallel-veined and consist of a blade and a sheath. The flowers are usually feathery or plumelike and feature an awn, or a barbed appendage, that is often quite long.

Ease of care: Easy.

How to grow: Unless specified, grasses need only a good, well-drained garden soil in full sun. A few will do equally well in moist or wet soil. The only chore connected with the perennial grasses is the annual pruning of the larger types in early spring. That is the time to cut the dead stems and leaves to within 6 inches of the ground before new growth begins. Division for the larger clumps is best effected with hearty digging and using an ax to divide the roots.

Sea Holly

Eryngium **species**
Zone: USDA 6

Propagation: By division in spring or by seed.
Uses: The large grasses make superb specimen plants. Both their seed heads and leaves provide interest until finally beaten down by winter snows. Ornamental grasses make excellent ground cover. The miscanthus grasses can also be used as valuable screens. Miscanthus types can also produce an astounding amount of flowers to be used in dried or winter bouquets.

Related species: *Calamagrostis acutiflora stricta,* or feather reed grass, reaches a height of 5 to 7 feet. It makes an upright stand of slender leaves and a narrow panicle up to 12 inches long that quickly turns a light tan. Although preferring sun, this grass will accept some open shade and will do well in damp situations. *Chasmanthium latifolium,* or sea oats (the genus means "gaping flower" in Greek), is one of the most valuable ornamental grasses that will do well in partial shade. It usually grows about 3 feet high. After the first frost, the leaves and flowers turn a rich, tannish-brown and remain on the plant well into December. If the flowers are picked while still green, they will retain their color. *Helictotrichon sempervirens,* or blue oat grass (the genus is Greek for "twisted awn"), is valuable for its blue color and the form of the leaves. It usually grows about 2 feet in height. The flowers are attractive. *Imperata cylindrica rubra,* or Japanese blood grass (the genus is named for *Ferrante Imperato*), consists of blades from 1 to 2 feet high that begin the season as green but quickly turn a deep, rich red. Happy in full sun or a bit of shade, the color is a startling addition to the flower garden

or the rock garden. In areas with winter temperatures below 0°F and a lack of snow, mulching is necessary. *Miscanthus sinensis* 'Gracillimus,' or maiden grass (Greek for "flower on a stalk"), varies from 5 to 8 feet in height, forming a tight clump of grass at ground level that quickly becomes a fountain of thin, arching leaves. In the fall, tall seed heads are formed that open into plumes persisting well into winter. The color is light tan after frost. *Miscanthus sinensis* 'Zebrinus,' or zebra grass, looks like a tropical plant that has adapted to the North. Reaching a height of 8 feet, the arching leaves are dashed with horizontal bands of a light and creamy golden-brown that only appears as the summer heats up. Massive clumps are formed over the years. Flowers are large and showy, tinted with an iridescent maroon until they open to silver, and eventually white. While full sun is required, zebra grass will persist in damp or dry soil and is an excellent waterside choice. *Pennisetum alopecuroides,* or fountain grass (Latin for "feathered bristles"), produces leafy fountains about 3 feet high and blossoms on arching stalks. These plants are best when planted singly rather than in masses.

Sea hollies resemble teasels, with compact heads of long-lasting, small blossoms surrounded by spiny petals that are actually leaves, or bracts. They belong to the carrot family, as evidenced by their thick tap roots. The genus is an ancient Greek name for a species of *Eryngium.*
Description: Sea hollies have simple, spiny-toothed leaves on stout stems from 2 to 6 feet tall, with clusters of teasel-like blossoms. They bloom in July and August.
Ease of care: Easy.
How to grow: Sea hollies need full sun and a good, well-drained soil worked to sufficient depth for the growth of the tap roots. Their deep roots make them difficult to transplant.
Propagation: By cuttings or by seed.
Uses: For a bold stroke in the formal garden or a fascinating addition to the wild garden, sea hollies are a good choice. The flowers are not only excellent when cut, they are also valuable when dried for winter bouquets.
Related species: *Eryngium alpinum* grows to 2 feet tall with 1¼-inch long, silvery-blue flower heads. 'Donardt's Blue' bears blue flowers on 2-foot stems. *Eryngium amethystinum* is one of the best species, bearing small, blue flowers on plants to 3 feet high. *Eryngium giganteum* grows to 3 or 4 feet with silver-blue flower heads to 2 inches long. This species dies after flowering, although it usually produces abundant seedlings. *Eryngium planum* has many round, ½-inch long, blue flowers on 3-foot stems. It is not as pretty as the other species, making it better suited in a wild garden.

Hosta, Plantain Lily

Hosta species
Zone: USDA 4

Next to daylilies, the most-common garden perennial plants are the hostas. The original species came from Korea, Japan, and China where they have been cultivated for centuries. The Japanese grow them in deep shade and full sun in pots, gardens, rock gardens, and temple gardens. They even use them cut up in stir-fry. In 1894, William Robinson called these plants *Funkia*. They were named in honor of Heinrich Christian Funck, a German doctor. By the turn of the century, the genus had been changed to *Hosta* in honor of Nicolaus Host, another German doctor. Both names still remain.

Description: Usually large clumps of basal leaves with pronounced veining and smooth or wavy edges distinguish hostas. Leaf colors come in various shades of green, often with many variegations. Lilylike flowers on tall stems (or scapes) in white and many shades of blue bloom from late spring to late summer.

Ease of care: Easy.

How to grow: Hostas do best in good, well-drained, moist garden soil with plenty of humus. They require some sun to partial shade to deep shade, depending on the species and variety. Many hostas can take a great deal of sun and adapt to dry spots in the garden. They dislike wet soil in winter. Once in place, hostas can survive for generations. The plants are very tough and only slugs present a problem that, if left unchecked, can produce large holes in the leaves.

Propagation: By division or by seed (some species).

Uses: There is a place in every garden for hostas. The smaller types are excellent in the border or as ground cover. The larger varieties become elegant specimen plants forming gigantic clumps of leaves over the years. Although usually grown for the leaves, the flowers are often beautiful, too. Hostas are the backbone of the shade garden, since many of them are happiest in full or open shade protected from the rays of the sun. They are also excellent in pots.

Related species: Some hosta suppliers will stock well over 200 different species and varieties of this adaptable plant. The following list is only a sampling of what's available, and the list grows every year. Those named enjoy shade to partial sun. *Hosta Fortunei* forms mounds about 14 inches high and 2 feet wide. It has oval leaves 5 inches wide and 12 inches long with pale purple flowers in early summer. 'Aureo-marginata' has a yellow-gold margin on a dark green leaf; 'Albo-marginata' has white edges on its leaves; and 'Albo-picta' has a bright yellow leaf with a crisp, dark green margin. *Hosta lancifolia* has small, spear-shaped, dark green leaves about 6 inches long, forming clumps about 1 foot high and 18 inches wide. Flowers are light purple on 22-inch stems blooming in summer. *Hosta montana* has dark green leaves 11 inches wide and up to 20 inches long, forming a mound 30 inches high and up to 4 feet wide. Flowers are off-white and bloom in early summer. 'Aureo-marginata' has wavy leaves of a glossy green with irregular, yellow margins. *Hosta plantaginea*, or the fragrant hosta, has large, heart-shaped leaves and produces sweet-smelling, white flowers in late summer or early autumn that can be killed by early frost if not protected. 'Grandiflora' has larger-than-species flowers in clumps that can reach 3 feet in diameter. *Hosta Sieboldiana* has round, blue-green, and seer-suckered leaves 12 inches wide and 14 inches long in mounds that can reach 30 inches high and 4 feet wide. 'Frances Williams' has blue-green leaves with broad, golden-yellow margins that deepen in color as the summer progresses. Lilac flowers appear in early summer. *Hosta Sieboldii* is a smaller plant with dark green, lance-shaped leaves a bit over 1 inch wide and 4 to 5 inches long. Flowers are white with purple veins and bloom in August. 'Kabitan' has leaves with a greenish-yellow base and a narrow, green margin. *Hosta undulata* has wavy leaves about 6 inches long and pale purple flowers in early summer. 'Variegata' has leaves with more white than green. *Hosta venusta* is a small plant from Korea with slightly wavy, green, heart-shaped leaves, 1 inch long and 1 inch wide. Flowers are violet and bloom in early summer.

Houttuynia

Houttuynia cordata
Zone: USDA 5

This plant became popular in the last few years. It is the only species in the genus and is named in honor of a Dutch naturalist. The plants are called *Dokudami* in Japan.

Description: Houttuynia resembles English ivy, with red stems and blue-green leaves somewhat metallic in appearance. It grows about 1 foot high and produces small, white flowers in summer that resemble begonia blossoms. When bruised, the plants smell of Seville oranges.

Ease of care: Easy.

How to grow: Plants grow well in sun and in shade but need good, well-drained garden soil that is always moist. Houttuynias will also grow in shallow water.

Propagation: By division or by seed.

Uses: These plants are a fine ground cover in beds, borders, and for the edge of a water garden. Plants spread by underground runners and can be quite invasive. Houttuynias adapt readily to potting.

Related varieties: 'Chameleon' has leaves variegated with blotches of green, red, yellow, and pink. 'Plena' has double flowers.

False Indigo, Wild Indigo

Baptisia australis
Zone: USDA 5

A beautiful plant in leaf, in flower, and after going to seed, false indigo was originally planted to produce a blue dye for early American colonists. Unfortunately, the dye wasn't fast. The name of the genus is from the Greek word for "dipping," which is also the root word for baptism.

Description: This is a large plant that grows to 4 feet in height. The blue-green, compound leaves on stout stems are attractive all summer, and the dark blue, pealike flowers that eventually become blackened pods are very showy.

Ease of care: Easy.

How to grow: It needs well-drained soil in full sun, but will accept some partial shade. Being a member of the legume family, baptisia will do well in poor soil. The root systems of older plants become so extensive that they are difficult to move.

Propagation: By division or by seed.

Uses: One baptisia will in time cover an area several feet in diameter with gracefully arching foliage. Because they die down to the ground in winter, a line of these plants makes a perfect deciduous hedge when spaced 3 feet apart. Because of the extensive root system, these plants are perfect for holding banks of soil in place. One plant makes a perfect specimen in the border. In addition, these plants are excellent for a meadow garden, a wild garden, or planted along the edge of the woods. The flowers are also beautiful when cut. After the fall frost, the leaves, as well as the inflated seedpods (often called Indian rattles), turn black. Expensive florist shops often gild these pods.

Related species: The prairie false indigo, *Baptisia leucantha*, has white flowers. It does well in the shade, although it is best in the wild garden as it's too rangy for a formal spot. *Baptisia perfoliata* is only reliably hardy to USDA Zone 7. The stems arch gracefully to the ground. The flowers are small and yellow, bloom in July, and appear surrounded by the gray-green leaves that resemble eucalyptus plants in growth habit. This plant is drought-resistant.

Inula

Inula ensifolia
Zone: USDA 4

Most gardeners think of the inulas as represented by elecampane (*Inula Helenium*), a large and raucous herb used in past centuries to heal both men and horses. But *I. ensifolia* is beautiful in the garden and available from most large nurseries.

Description: Inula is a clump-forming plant with thin, narrow leaves on thin stems growing to 16 inches, topped with bright yellow, 1½-inch wide daisies. They bloom in July and August.

Ease of care: Easy.

How to grow: Inulas want only a sunny spot in good garden soil in order to succeed. Seeds sown in early spring will bloom the first year.

Propagation: By division or by seed.

Uses: These yellow daisies are perfect for the front of a bed or border and also make excellent cut flowers.

Related variety: 'Gold Star' produces flowers up to 2½ inches wide.

Iris

Iris **species**
Zone: USDA 4

Just as gardeners could create a fascinating garden using nothing but daylilies and hostas, the same approach would also work for the iris. This large genus contains over 200 species in the northern hemisphere and is most abundant in Asia. The plants are responsible for a marvelous array of flowers plus, in many cases, fine foliage.

Description: Irises usually have basal leaves in two ranks, linear to sword-shaped, often resembling a fan, arising from a thick rootstock (or rhizome) or, in some species, from a bulb. There are three groups in the rhizomatous species: Bearded iris has a "beard" or pattern of hairs on the bottom half of the falls (the lower petals); the crested iris has a cockscomblike crest on the falls; and the beardless iris has no hairs on the bottom petals. They come in shades of pink, blue, lilac, purple to brown, yellow, orange, dark to almost black, and white. There are no true reds.

Ease of care: Easy.

How to grow: Most irises need sunlight. Except for those like the water flag (*Iris Pseudacorus*) that delights in a watery spot or the Japanese iris (*I. ensata*) that wants a humus-rich, moist soil, they also prefer a good, well-drained garden soil. In the North, rhizomatous irises should have the tops of the rhizome showing when planted; in the South, they should be covered slightly. The fan of leaves is to be pointed in the direction you wish the plants to grow.

Propagation: By division in the fall or by seed.

Uses: Even though bloom period is short, a bed of irises is ideal for a flower garden. There are irises for the poolside and the pool, the wild or woodland garden, the early spring bulb bed, and the rock garden.

Related species: Tall, bearded iris, hardy to USDA 4, sometimes called *Iris germanica*, usually comes to mind when people think of irises. The flowers come in a multitude of color combinations and sizes, with hundreds of new varieties introduced every year. The fanlike leaves are a lovely gray-green, browning at the tips in a hot summer. There are varieties that bloom both in the spring and the fall. Tall bearded irises are over 25 inches tall; intermediate bearded ones are between 16 and 27 inches tall; the standard plants are between 8 and 16 inches, and the miniatures grow to 8 inches tall. As with daylilies and hostas, there is a bewildering number of varieties and colors. Perhaps the best suggestion for the beginning gardener is to order a mix of colors, a choice frequently offered by most nurseries. *Iris cristata*, the dwarf, crested iris that is hardy in USDA 5, wants partial shade and a humus-rich soil and blooms in early spring. It is lavender-blue with a 2-inch, yellow crest across a 6-inch stem. The leaves are attractive after bloom. In areas of bad winters with little snow, these plants need mulching. 'Alba' is white and 'Summer Storm' is deep blue. *Iris foetidissima*, or the Gladwin iris, has a distinct smell of roast beef or boiled meat when bruised and does not deserve its other common name of "stinking gladdon." Hardy to USDA 6 and doing best in good soil in partial shade, it is grown for its seedpods on 18-inch stems which, upon bursting open in autumn, reveal beautiful orange-red shining seeds that are used for indoor arrangements. *Iris Kaempferi* is the nursery name for the Japanese iris, and *I. ensata* is the official botanical term. They are hardy in USDA 6. Blossoms are often over 6 inches wide on stiff, 8-inch stems, blooming in June and resembling layers of colored linen

Knapweed

Centaurea **species**
Zone: USDA 4

Knotweed, Himalaya Fleece Flower

Polygonum affine
Zone: USDA 4

waving in the wind. Plants prefer evenly moist soil and do well near the water's edge. There are many color choices: 'Gold Bound' is a double white with a golden band on each petal; 'Eleanor Parry' has reddish-purple flowers; and 'Great White Heron' is a white, semi-double up to 11 inches in diameter. The Higo Strain from Japan includes 'Nikko' with petals of pale purple-blue and a gold throat. *Iris pallida*, or the orris iris, grown primarily for foliage, produces flowers on 3-foot stems with fragrant, lilac flowers. It is hardy in USDA 6 and prefers partial shade. 'Albo-Variegata' has white-striped leaves and 'Variegata' has yellow, vertical stripes. *Iris Pseudacorus*, the yellow flag, is a beautiful plant for the bog or at the edge of a pond or pool. The flowers, blooming in late May to June, are yellow on 40-inch stems. 'Light Yellow' is lemon-colored, and 'Flore Plena' has double, yellow flowers. *Iris pumila*, the dwarf bearded iris, grows 4 to 6 inches high, blooming in early May, and is suited for the rock garden in full sun. 'Blue Frost' has light blue flowers; 'Red Dandy' is a wine-red; and 'Golden Fair' is a deep gold. *Iris sibirica*, the Siberian iris, is a plant that has beautiful 3- to 4-inch flowers on 30-inch stems and great foliage—the swordlike leaves stand erect and eventually form a large clump. They need full sun, prefer a good, moist soil, and are hardy in USDA 4. 'Blue Brilliant' is as named; 'Ruffled Velvet' has deep plum-purple flowers; and 'Snow Queen' is pure white. *Iris tectorum*, the Japanese roof iris, is supposedly used as a living binding material for thatched roofs in the Orient. Plants are hardy in USDA 5; grow about 1 foot high; and are covered in June with 6-inch, lilac-blue flowers. Soil should be good and moist, with mulch used in areas without winter snow. 'Alba' is white.

Four useful garden perennials—*Centaurea dealbata, Centaurea hypoleuca, Centaurea macrocephala*, and *Centaurea montana*—belong to this genus, all resembling the popular annual bachelor's buttons. The genus derives its name from a species, which, according to mythology, was used to cure the foot of a Greek centaur called Chiron.
Description: Knapweed has large leaves; the usually stout-stemmed plants bear thistlelike flowers.
Ease of care: Easy.
How to grow: Knapweeds like full sun and any good garden soil that is dry and well drained.
Propagation: By division or by seed.
Uses: Grouped in the border or set throughout the garden, these flowers are bright and cheerful, bearing attractive seed heads.
Related species: *Centaurea dealbata*, or the Persian knapweed, bears bright, rose-purple flowers typical of the genus that bloom over a long period on 2-foot stems. The coarsely cut leaves are gray and hairy underneath and green on top. Plants sometimes need staking. *Centaurea hypoleuca* blooms from June to August with 2- to 3-inch flowers of rich rose on 18-inch stems. Leaves are green above and silvery white beneath. The seed heads are very attractive. *Centaurea macrocephala* has no common name. The plants have large, coarse leaves with stout stems often reaching 4 feet in height. The blossoms are bright yellow and resemble thistles. They make good cut flowers and are excellent when dried. They only bloom for a short time. *Centaurea montana*, or the mountain bluet, has cornflower-blue flowers that bloom over a long period on 18-inch stems. Young foliage is silvery white.

One of the most pernicious weeds in America is the so-called Japanese bamboo, *Polygonum cuspidatum*, a plant that is as happy along a roadside as it is in a garden. Luckily, the plant described below is small and attractive. The genus name is from the Greek for "many knees," referring to the large number of joints found on the stems.
Description: Himalaya fleece flower is a tufted ground cover plant with dark green, tapered leaves on creeping stems. Tiny, bright rose flowers bloom in dense spikes about 8 inches high from late summer into fall.
Ease of care: Easy.
How to grow: Knotweed requires good soil, preferably slightly moist, in full sun.
Propagation: By division in spring.
Uses: The plant is good as a ground cover or as an edging plant for the bed or border. It is especially valuable because the plant sends up new flowers over a long period.
Related species: *Polygonum Bistorta* 'Superbum' is a very attractive plant for the border that bears 6-inch pinkish spikes of flowers on 2-foot stems. Plants prefer light shade in areas with hot summers. Soil should be moist. *Polygonum cuspidatum* var. *compactum* is a dwarf form of Japanese bamboo that grows under 2 feet in height, wants full sun, and makes a good ground cover.
Related varieties: 'Darjeeling Red' has pale pink flowers when new, turning to a deep rose-red as they mature; 'Donald Lowndes' has flowers of a light pink.

Ladybells

Adenophora confusa
Zone: USDA 4

Ladybells are often confused with campanulas, although they do differ in subtle botanical characteristics. *Adenophora* refers to small glands that circle the female parts of the flower. The species name underscores the botanical confusion in identification. They originally came from China and Korea.

Description: Tall, 30-inch spires of dark blue, bell-shaped flowers bloom in mid- to late summer. These flowers are often found in old gardens as they persist for years.

Ease of care: Easy.

How to grow: Ladybells are easy to grow, but their fleshy roots defy division. Since they can only be moved when they are dormant, their garden location must be chosen with care. As with any plant that is expected to occupy the same spot for its lifetime, ladybells must be provided with a good, deep, well-drained garden soil that remains moist but never wet. Plants need full sun or partial shade.

Propagation: By cuttings or by seed.

Uses: Ladybells have such beautiful blue flowers that they are welcome additions to the summer garden. They are also excellent for the woodland garden.

Related species: *Adenophora liliifolia* is sometimes offered by dealers. The flowers are pale blue on 2-foot stems.

Lady's Mantle

Alchemilla species
Zone: USDA 3b

Lady's mantles are beautiful plants usually grown for both their foliage and the unusual chartreuse flowers. The botanical name is a Latinized term for an old Arabic name.

Description: Plants grow between 8 and 14 inches high, with lobed leaves of gray-green that bear silky hairs.

Ease of care: Easy.

How to grow: Lady's mantles are easy to grow in average garden soil where summers are cool and moist, preferring some protection from hot sun in midsummer. In warmer parts of the country, they need a moist, fertile soil and light shade. As the summer progresses, the plants become larger and have a tendency to flop about. Flowers should be removed before the seeds ripen, as they can seed about.

Propagation: By division in spring or by seed.

Uses: The flowers appear in clusters in early summer, standing well above the leaves, and last for several weeks. They are excellent when cut. These plants can be used in the front of the garden border or along the edge of a low wall where the leaves are easy to see.

Related species: Three species are usually offered: *Alchemilla alpina,* the alpine lady's mantle, grows about 8 inches high; *Alchemilla erythropoda* grows about 6 inches high; and *Alchemilla mollis,* the most common, grows to 14 inches high.

Lamb's-Ears, Lamb's-Tongue

Stachys byzantina
Zone: USDA 5

Some plants beg to have a finger run along their surface; among such plants, lamb's-ear is one of the best. The common name is precisely on the mark, since the gray-white, woolly leaves feel exactly like a lamb's skin. The genus name is Greek for "a spike of grain."

Description: The 4-inch-long leaves and sturdy stems of this plant are covered with dense, white wool. Plants grow to about 6 inches tall. Flower spikes up to 2 feet tall bear small, pink to purple flowers hidden by silvery bracts.

Ease of care: Easy.

How to grow: Lamb's-ears require full sun and a good, well-drained soil. They are drought-resistant.

Propagation: By division in spring or by seed.

Uses: Try this plant along the edge of a sunny border, in the rock garden, or as an effective ground cover. Even though the flowers are insignificant, the dried spikes are very effective in dried arrangements. It also does well in pots for terrace decoration.

Related variety: 'Silver Carpet' is a nonflowering form of the same plant.

Lavender

Lavandula angustifolia
Zone: USDA 4

These are species of aromatic herbs originally from the Mediterranean. The genus name is from the word *lava*, which originally referred to a torrential downpour of rain and then became the word *lavare*, "to wash." It alludes to the ancient custom of scenting bath water with oil of lavender or a few lavender flowers.
Description: Plants are shrubby, usually with square stems and narrow, evergreen leaves that are white and woolly when young. Flower spikes have terminal clusters of lavender or dark purple flowers, blooming in late June and bearing a pleasing scent.
Ease of care: Easy.
How to grow: Lavender plants want full sun and well-drained, sandy soil—preferably not acid. In areas where there is no snow cover, the plants should be mulched. In colder areas, prune back the dead wood in the spring.
Propagation: By soft cuttings in spring or by seed.
Uses: Lavender is perfect as a low hedge and in clumps next to rocks. It is also suitable in front of stone walls that face away from the wind.
Related varieties: 'Hidcote' has deep violet flowers on 20-inch shrubs; 'Munstead Dwarf,' a shorter type, has deep purple flowers at a 12-inch height.

Sea Lavender

Limonium latifolium
Zone: USDA 4

There are many annuals in this genus—flowers that are dried and used in winter bouquets. But one perennial, *Limonium latifolium*, is especially effective for its branching sprays of tiny flowers that resemble baby's breath in character. The genus name is from the Greek word for "meadow" and refers to the frequent occurrence of some species in salt meadows.
Description: Large, leathery leaves to 10 inches long form a basal rosette, which, in late July and August, sends up 2-foot stems that branch out into huge clouds of tiny ⅛-inch lavender-blue flowers.
Ease of care: Easy.
How to grow: Plants need full sun and a good, well-drained garden soil with plenty of sand for drainage. They do well in seaside gardens.
Propagation: By division or by seed.
Uses: Since they bloom in summer, sea lavenders are excellent choices for beds and borders where their airy cloud of flowers has a lovely effect.
Related variety: 'Violette' has brilliant, violet-blue flowers that keep their color when dried.

Leopard's-bane

Doronicum cordatum
Zone: USDA 5

All the plants in this genus were once thought to be poisonous to animals, hence the common name of "leopard's-bane." The genus is from an old Arabic name for the flowers. Some catalogs list it as *Doronicum caucasicum*.
Description: Bright yellow, daisylike flowers bloom 2 inches across, reaching a height of up to 2 feet. Leaves are heart-shaped with a toothed edge; they clasp the stems. Plants bloom in the spring.
Ease of care: Easy.
How to grow: Leopard's-banes prefer a good, well-drained soil in partial shade. Since their roots are shallow, they also benefit from a moist situation. These plants prefer cool summers. In hot climates, they must have some shade.
Propagation: By division in early spring or by seed.
Uses: Since these flowers bloom in spring and usually go dormant by midsummer, they should be planted where their absence will not be missed. They make fine border plants when massed and are beautiful in front of a low wall. They also make excellent cut flowers.
Related varieties: 'Magnificum' has larger-than-average heads, and 'Finesse' bears bright yellow blooms 3 inches in diameter on 18-inch stems.

Ligularia

Ligularia species
Zone: USDA 4 to 6

The plant's name comes from the Latin word *ligula*, which means "little tongue," and refers to the tonguelike shape of the large petal on each of the ray flowers.

Description: Basal leaves on stout stems are either round or kidney-shaped. They bear tall spires of yellow or orange flower heads. The flowers smell of chocolate.

Ease of care: Easy.

How to grow: Ligularias do best in partial shade and good, humus-rich garden soil that is kept evenly moist. Even with plenty of water, the leaves will wilt in hot summer heat, but they quickly recover as the sun sets and temperatures fall. Since the roots form large clumps, plenty of space should be allowed between plants.

Propagation: By division in spring or by seed.

Uses: Ligularias are great in the back of shady beds, along borders, in bogs, or planted at the edge of water gardens.

Related species: *Ligularia dentata* 'Orange Queen' and 'Othello' each has leaves up to 1 foot wide. The first is green throughout with flowers of a deeper orange, while the second has leaves that are green on top and purple underneath. *Ligularia Przewalskii* 'The Rocket' and *Ligularia stenocephala* 'The Rocket' both bloom in late July and early August with large, serrated leaves and tall spires of bright yellow flowers on purple stems. *Ligularia tussilaginea* 'Aureo-maculata' has leaves splotched with areas of yellow or white. It is hardy only to USDA 7. *Ligularia Veitchiana* forms large clumps that can reach 7 feet if growing conditions are good. Flower heads are bright orange and are about 2½ inches across.

Blackberry Lily, Leopard Lily

Belamcanda chinensis
Zone: USDA 6 (zone 5 with protection)

Belamcanda is an East Indian name for this genus of irislike plants that are native to China, Japan, and Korea. They have escaped from gardens and are now established in pastures and along roadsides in many northeastern states.

Description: Blackberry lilies have 10-inch long, sword-shaped leaves that give rise to 2-foot stems. Each stem holds many 6-petaled, orange flowers speckled with red. Flowers only last for a day, drying with a twist into tight spirals, then falling as pods develop. They are, however, soon followed by other blossoms, flowering during July and August. Eventually the oval, green pods split open to reveal attractive, shiny black seeds.

Ease of care: Easy.

How to grow: Belamcandas prefer well-drained and fertile soil in full sun. They resent heavy clay soils where the roots have a tendency to rot.

Propagation: By division of the rhizomes in early spring or by seed.

Uses: A large grouping of these plants looks especially attractive when backed by a stone wall or in company with gooseneck plants (*Lysimachia clethroides*) or planted among mounds of two ornamental grasses.

Related species: *Belamcanda flabellata* has 8-inch leaves and bears yellow flowers. 'Hello Yellow' grows to 15 inches.

Related variety: 'Freckle Face' produces flowers of a light orange that bloom the first year if planted early.

Toad Lily

Tricyrtis hirta
Zone: USDA 5b

It's unfortunate that such an attractive and unusual flower should have the common name of "toad lily." The amphibian reference really refers to the blotches and markings on the flowers. The genus name is from the Greek for "three" and "convex" because the 3 outer petals have tiny bags or swellings at the base.

Description: Plants have alternate, 6-inch leaves on arching, hairy stems that are usually 2 feet high. They bear single, creamy white flowers, often in clusters, which open to purple-spotted petals and centers resembling pieces of chenille. They usually bloom in late September or October.

Ease of care: Moderately easy.

How to grow: Toad lilies need a moist, fertile soil with a high humus content and partial shade, or the open shade found beneath trees. In higher elevations of Zone 5b where fall frosts arrive early, the plants must be protected.

Propagation: By seed or by division in spring.

Uses: Toad lilies should be planted where they are easily seen. The plants are especially valuable for the shade garden and are among the few that bloom so late in the garden year.

Related species: *Tricyrtis formosana* has flowers spotted with mauve on a lighter background with yellow in the throat.

Big Blue Lily Turf

Liriope Muscari
Zone: USDA 6

Lily turf is a grasslike plant belonging to the lily family. It is often used as a low-maintenance ground cover in institutional landscapes. The genus name is derived from Liriope, who was the mother of Narcissus.

Description: Firm, evergreen, grasslike leaves, often over 1 foot long, grow in tufts. They produce terminal spikes of small flowers that bloom in late summer with violet or dark blue flowers, which are followed by glossy black seeds.

Ease of care: Easy.

How to grow: Liriopes respond well to any good, well-drained garden soil either in sun or shade. They require no special care.

Propagation: By division in early spring.

Uses: Liriopes are unexcelled as a ground cover. They are also excellent along paths and walkways or massed in the front of a border, where their evergreen leaves are attractive in the fall and winter.

Related varieties: 'Christmas Tree' has larger-than-type lavender flowers on 8-inch plants; 'Majestic' grows to a 15-inch height with large, deep lilac flowers; and 'Monroe's White' is 12 inches high with white flowers.

Gooseneck Loosestrife

Lysimachia clethroides
Zone: USDA 5

Few plants deserve such a descriptive common name as this particular species does—a number of them in bloom truly look like a gaggle of geese ready to honk at an intruder. The genus is named after King Lysimachus of Thrace.

Description: Gooseneck loosestrifes have alternate, simple leaves on stout stems that grow to 3 feet tall. They end in nodding whorls of small, white flowers that bloom in the summer.

Ease of care: Easy.

How to grow: This particular member of the loosestrifes prefers a good, well-drained, moist soil in full sun or partial shade. If the site is to its liking, it will quickly spread—so contain the roots if necessary.

Propagation: By division or by seed.

Uses: Put these plants in a moist part of the bed or border or use them unrestrained in the wild garden. They are also excellent cut flowers.

Related species: *Lysimachia punctata,* or the garden loosestrife, is an old-fashioned garden plant with bright yellow flowers that whorl around the stem among the leaves. Height is between 2 and 3 feet, blooming in early summer. It will tolerate drier soil if given partial shade.

Purple Loosestrife

Lythrum Salicaria
Zone: USDA 4

Purple loosestrife has become naturalized throughout the Northeast, especially in marshy lands. The genus name comes from the Greek word for "gore" and refers to the dark color of some flowers.

Description: Purple loosestrifes have strong stems growing to 6 feet high with willowlike leaves and flowers in terminal spikes. They grow best in boggy and wet places.

Ease of care: Easy.

How to grow: Preferring moist soil in full sun, loosestrifes will easily adapt to streamside planting, as the roots can grow in water. They can also adapt to a fairly dry spot in the shade.

Propagation: By division.

Uses: For naturalizing in the wild garden or for beautiful color in the August border, loosestrifes are excellent.

Related varieties: 'Dropmore Purple' has rich purple flowers, while 'Moden's Pink' are of rose-pink—both are on 3-foot stems; 'Fire-candle' (sometimes called 'Feuerkerze') has blossoms of an intense rosy-red. 'Robert' bears rose-red flowers to a height of 18 to 24 inches, with foliage turning scarlet in the fall.

Lungwort, Jerusalem Sage

Pulmonaria officinalis
Zone: USDA 4

One of the first flowers of spring, the lungworts are exceptional plants for both their blossoms and foliage. Because the leaves are dotted with white spots, the plant was thought to be a medicine for lungs. The genus name is from the Latin word for "lung."

Description: Lungworts have simple basal leaves growing to 1 foot long, which are spotted with silver-white splotches. Terminal coiled clusters of 5-lobed flowers, which in many species open as pink and then fade with age to blue, bloom in the spring.

Ease of care: Easy.

How to grow: While lungworts will persist in poor soil, they are truly lovely when planted in a good, moist garden soil in partial to full shade. Water must be provided during times of drought.

Propagation: By division in fall or by seed.

Uses: Lungworts are lovely plants for the shade garden, the wild garden, and even as ground covers on banks under the shadow of trees and bushes. Plants can be potted in late fall and forced into greenhouse bloom.

Related species: *Pulmonaria angustifolia* 'Azurea' is a European plant that bears brilliant blue flowers; 'Johnson's Blue' has gentian-blue flowers. *Pulmonaria montana*, often called *P. rubra*, has plain green leaves and bears salmon-red flowers. *Pulmonaria saccharata*, or the Bethlehem sage, is usually represented by 'Mrs. Moon,' which has very attractive leaf spotting; 'Janet Fisk' has much silver in its foliage. 'Sissinghurst White' bears white flowers.

Lupine

Lupinus polyphyllus
Zone: USDA 5

Some authorities think that *Lupinus* comes from the Latin word for "wolf," as it was an ancient belief that lupines destroyed the fertility of the soil. Others, however, think the name is from the Greek *lype* for "bitter," because the seeds have a bitter taste and were considered a food of the downtrodden.

Description: Attractive alternate, gray-green leaves are fingerlike, with many leaflets beginning at a central point. In early summer, plants produce 30-inch spikes of pealike flowers followed by silky seedpods.

Ease of care: Moderately easy.

How to grow: Lupines require a lot of water and a spot in full sun or in the lightest of shade. Plants resent areas with hot summers. Soil must be well-drained with additional grit or sand. Lupines do not adapt to alkaline soil. Remove the dead flowers to prevent seed formation and to conserve the plant's strength. Cutting back to the ground after flowering will often produce a second crop of blossoms.

Propagation: By seed or division in early spring.

Uses: Lupines should be planted in large groups where their flowers make a spectacular sight. The plants are especially suited to seaside gardens.

Related varieties: The Russell strain of lupines are the variety that is usually offered by nurseries. They can be purchased in mixed colors that include blue, pink, red, purple, maroon, white, and mixed colors. Some nurseries offer individual colors.

Carolina Lupine, Aaron's Rod

Thermopsis caroliniana
Zone: USDA 4

Carolina lupines are native American wildflowers originally from North Carolina and Georgia. They closely resemble *Baptisia australis*; both are members of the pea family. The genus is Greek for "resembling a lupine."

Description: Leaves have 3 leaflets on stems growing to 5 feet and bear spikes of yellow, pealike flowers in late June and July, followed by pods resembling small string beans that are covered with short hairs.

Ease of care: Easy.

How to grow: Plants grow in almost any good, well-drained soil in full sun. Without full sun, the stems will lean to the light and then flop over. In rich soil, plants will be very tall and need staking. New plants take a few years to form sizable clumps. If given adequate moisture just before flowering begins, plants are very drought-resistant.

Propagation: By division in early spring or by seed.

Uses: The spikes of yellow flowers are very attractive against a dark background, so keep them at the back of the border, especially in front of bushes or shrubbery. They bloom at a time of the garden year when yellows are mostly absent. The light green leaves remain attractive until frost.

Related species: *Thermopsis montana* grows to 2 feet.

Mallow

Malva Alcea
Zone: USDA 4

Malvas are lovely flowers that bloom in late summer and into fall. *Malva* is the ancient Latin name for "mallow," used by Pliny and derived from the Greek name *Malachi*, "to soften," in reference to its emollient qualities.
Description: Mallow is a bushy perennial with stout stems growing to 4 feet. Soft green, fingered leaves and 5-petaled flowers in the leaf axils bloom over a long period.
Ease of care: Easy.
How to grow: Malvas are not fussy about soil, and any good garden soil will do. They adapt to dry conditions, but do require full sun or, at best, a bit of shade.
Propagation: By seed or by division in early spring.
Uses: Malvas mix beautifully with white phlox and in the midst of ornamental grasses. They are most effective when planted mid-border.
Related species: *Malva moschata* 'Alba' is similar to *M. Alcea*, with white flowers on slightly shorter stems.
Related variety: 'Fastigiata' has pink flowers with darker veining. It requires no staking and can be used for cut flowers.

Rose Mallow, Swamp Mallow

Hibiscus Moscheutos
Zone: USDA 5

This native American genus contains many plants including roselle (*Hibiscus Sabdariffa*), from which carcade, a beverage that Mussolini wanted the Italians to drink, is made. *Hibiscus* is Latin for "marsh mallow."
Description: Hollyhocklike flowers up to 10 inches across bloom in pink, purple, or white with a dark red eye. Plants have alternate leaves, green above and white and hairy beneath, on stems to 7 feet in height. Plants bloom most of the summer.
Ease of care: Easy.
How to grow: Rose mallows prefer good, moist garden soil in full sun, but the plants will adapt to dry soil. All the members of the clan make big clumps in time, so plenty of room for growth must be allowed. The mallows seem to be unaffected by salt, making them an excellent choice along highways. Without a snow cover, a mulch must be provided in cold areas.
Propagation: By division or by seed.
Uses: Mallows are fine for wild gardens and places with damp soil. They are also excellent for the back of a bed or border and can easily be grown in pots. When planted in groups, the flowers will make the backyard look like a tropical paradise.
Related species: *Hibiscus coccineus* bears bright red flowers on 4-foot plants and is native to the southern United States. It is not hardy north of Philadelphia.
Related varieties: 'Southern Belle' produces huge flowers often up to 10 inches across in colors of red, rose, pink, and white on 4-foot plants. 'Poinsettia' is a rich red, and 'Silver Rose' is pink. Both reach 5 feet in height.

Meadowsweet, Queen-of-the-Prairie

Filipendula rubra
Zone: USDA 3

Meadowsweet is an American native at home at the edge of woods, in wet prairies, and in meadows from New York to Minnesota and south. A member of the rose family, the genus name means "hanging by a thread" and is said to refer to tubers that hang on the roots of one species.
Description: Meadowsweet is a tall plant, growing to 7 feet with large clusters of tiny, pink flowers. Together they are reminiscent of a ball of cotton candy. They sit on top of stout stems and bloom in July.
Ease of care: Easy.
How to grow: Meadowsweets prefer a good, well-drained, moist garden soil in full sun, although they will succeed in partial shade. Plants eventually form a good-sized clump.
Propagation: By division in early spring or by seed.
Uses: Meadowsweet is best toward the back of a border and against a dark background such as low trees or shrubs.
Related species: *Filipendula purpurea* 'Elegans,' sometimes listed as *F. palmata*, is from Japan. Plants reach between 30 and 40 inches in height and bear pale pink flowers in clusters, blooming in July. *Filipendula Ulmaria* grows between 3 and 5 feet tall. Flowers resemble feathery plumes and appear in June. 'Plena' grows to 3 feet, with double flowers, and 'Variegated' has green leaves with creamy yellow stripes in the center. *Filipendula vulgaris*, or *F. hexapetala*, has finely cut leaves and bears loose panicles of small, white flowers on 18-inch stems, blooming in June. 'Flore Pleno' has double flowers.

Dead Nettle

Lamium maculatum
Zone: USDA 5

The nettles are generally weedy plants, with only this genus valued for the garden. The term "dead" refers to the fact that these perennials do not cause pain in the manner usually reserved for the stinging nettles (*Utrica dioica*), plants which they somewhat resemble. *Lamium* is the ancient Latin name for plants in this genus.

Description: Dead nettles are sprawling plants with square stems, toothed oval leaves, and 1-inch long flowers that resemble small snapdragons. They bloom in May and June.

Ease of care: Easy.

How to grow: Lamiums are not fussy, doing well in a good, well-drained garden soil. They are more robust in partial shade and moist soil, yet they are reasonably drought-resistant.

Propagation: By division in spring.

Uses: Lamiums are excellent ground covers and border edgings both in the formal garden or the wild or woodland garden. Their variegated leaves are as attractive as the flowers.

Related varieties: 'Aureum' has a golden leaf with a white center and lavender-pink flowers; 'Album' has dark green leaves with silvery white splotches; 'Beacon Silver' has leaves of a silvery green with dark green edges and pink flowers; 'Chequers' has deep pink flowers and marbled leaves; and 'White Nancy' is a white-flowered form of 'Beacon Silver.'

Obedient Plant, False Dragonhead

Physostegia virginiana
Zone: USDA 4

A member of the mint family, obedient plants are native American wildflowers, still called *Dracocephalum* in some reference books. The genus name is from the Greek for "swollen bladder" and refers to the inflated body of the flower.

Description: Basal rosettes are evergreen in milder climates. Square, strong stems are from 1 to 3 feet tall and have narrow, toothed leaves, bearing rose-purple flowers that resemble a snapdragon. The individual flowers can be pushed around the stem without harm and will remain pointing in the same direction as when last touched.

Ease of care: Easy.

How to grow: Plants like full sun and will tolerate most soils, preferring the addition of some organic matter. They are at their best in moist conditions. The common types are invasive and should be either fenced at ground level or divided every two years.

Propagation: By division in spring or by seed.

Uses: Because they flower late in the season, these are valuable plants for beds and borders. They will often bloom into October. They should be planted in groups and are excellent for naturalizing in the wild garden.

Related varieties: 'Alba' is pure white and blooms in late summer on 24-inch stems; 'Bouquet Rose' has rose-colored flowers on 3-foot stems; and 'Vivid' stays about 15 inches high with flowers of a brilliant lavender-pink.

Ox-Eye, False Sunflower

Heliopsis helianthoides
Zone: USDA 5

Ox-eyes are native American plants found from New York to Michigan and south to Georgia. Members of the daisy family, they are similar to sunflowers but bloom earlier in the season. The genus is Greek for "like the sun."

Description: Ox-eyes are bright yellow daisies, often 4 inches in diameter on stout stems that grow between 3 and 5 feet tall. The leaves are simple and toothed. Flowers bloom from summer to frost.

Ease of care: Easy.

How to grow: These plants will bloom the first year from seed. Although they want full sun, ox-eyes will tolerate partial shade. They need a good, well-drained garden soil and will require extra water during periods of drought.

Propagation: By division in spring or by seed.

Uses: Since their cheerful flowers bloom over such a long period, ox-eyes are valuable in a bed, a border, and in a wild garden. The flowers are excellent for cutting.

Related species: *Heliopsis scabra* is a subspecies sometimes offered by nurseries.

Related varieties: 'Gold Greenheart' has double, yellow-green flowers with a green center when newly opened. 'Golden Plume' has double, yellow flowers about 2½ inches across.

Pachysandra, Japanese Spurge

Pachysandra terminalis
Zone: USDA 5

Pachysandra is the quintessential ground cover. The genus name is from the Greek and means "a thick man," in reference to the filaments in the flower.

Description: Fleshy stems about 1 foot high have simple, toothed, evergreen leaves. These are often crowded at the tips of branches, which bear small, greenish-white flowers in erect spikes in the spring.

Ease of care: Easy.

How to grow: Any good, moist garden soil is sufficient for pachysandra. The plants are especially valuable since they will grow in shady areas where few other plants survive. The leaves will yellow in full sun.

Propagation: By division or by cuttings.

Uses: Pachysandra is great under bushes and in the open shade found under evergreen trees. It can be used to carpet banks and as edging along shaded walkways. Plants can also be set in pots for the terrace.

Related species: *Pachysandra procumbens,* or Allegheny spurge, is a native American wildflower that is usually evergreen as far north as Zone 5. Stems have a purplish tinge and bear toothed leaves flecked with silver that becomes more pronounced in the spring. The spring flowers are off-white and quite beautiful. Good soil should have additional humus.

Related variety: 'Silver Edge' has a narrow, silvery white edge around the light, toothed, green leaves.

Perennial Pea, Sweet Pea

Lathyrus latifolius
Zone: USDA 5

These vines are perennial wildflowers imported from Europe and now naturalized over much of the Northeast. The word *Lathyrus* is Latin for a "thick pottage" and refers to the use of pea seeds in porridge.

Description: Perennial pea is a vining plant with paired leaflets of light green with winged stems. It bears tendrils and sweet-pealike flowers of pink, bluish-red, or white and blooms in August.

Ease of care: Easy.

How to grow: Perennial peas do well in any good garden soil, often reaching a length of 10 feet in one season. In fact, they sometimes do too well and can become a garden pest.

Propagation: By division or by seed.

Uses: They are perfect for ground covers, especially for hard-to-plant slopes and banks. They also grow on trellises. The flowers are excellent when cut.

Related varieties: 'Albus' has white flowers, and 'Splendens' has dark, reddish-purple flowers.

Peony

Paeonia species
Zone: USDA 5

Not only are peony flowers beautiful, the plants are especially attractive, too. Throughout history, peonies have been famous—they have inspired poetry, been the subjects for tapestry and wall paintings, and been included in witches' brews. They are named for the Greek physician Paeon, who first used the plants for medicinal purposes.

Description: Herbaceous peonies are shrubby plants with thick roots and large, compound, glossy green leaves on reddish stems. They bear large, many petaled, showy flowers with a pleasing fragrance. They bloom in June and are followed by large, interesting seedpods. Ants are often seen in company with peony buds. Herbaceous peonies die down to the ground for the winter. Tree peonies have branches with obvious bark. Like small trees, tree peonies remain in evidence all year and should not be cut down.

Ease of care: Easy.

How to grow: Autumn planting is best. This means full sun (except in the South) and a proper hole with good, well-drained, moisture-retentive soil rich with humus. If soil is excessively acid, add one cup of lime per plant. Keep manure and added fertilizers away from direct contact with the roots. Plant with the "eyes" or growing points to the top about 1½ inch below the soil surface. Water well. Mulch the first year to protect from severe cold.

Propagation: By division of the roots or by seed (seedlings will take 3 years or more to bloom).

Uses: As specimen plants, in hedges, beds or borders, and even in the cutting garden, peonies should be an important part of any garden. Remember that even if they did not bloom, the attractive shape and gloss of the

(continued)

Peony (continued)

leaves and their shrubby aspect would make them valuable.

Related species: *Paeonia Mlokosewitschii,* or the Caucasian peony, bears yellow flowers about 5 inches across. *Paeonia suffruticosa* is the Japanese tree peony (originally Chinese but refined—not discovered—by the Japanese), which is actually a bush, usually reaching a height of 5 feet and a spread of 6 feet. Flowers are between 6 and 8 inches across. 'Chinese Dragon' has semi-double blossoms of a rich crimson; 'Age of Gold' has large, double, golden blossoms; and 'Gauguin' has yellow petals inked with rose-red lines.

Related varieties: Various crosses of peony species have led to a large number of double varieties. According to type, they will bloom early, midseason, or late in June. Some of the more attractive are 'Bowl of Cream,' with pure white, double blossoms 8 inches across, blooming in midseason; 'Emma Klehm,' with double, deep pink flowers that bloom late in the season; 'Coral Sunset,' with flowers of intense coral, blooming early; and 'Sarah Bernhardt,' which has deep pink petals, lighter toward the edge, with a marvelous fragrance. It blooms late in the season.

Periwinkle, Myrtle

Vinca minor
Zone: USDA 5

This charming plant has a long history. Originally a native of southern Europe, plants were brought over by the colonists, and now it has naturalized over much of the Northeast. "Periwinkle" is thought to be an old Slavic word, *pervinka,* meaning "first" and referring to the early spring flowers.

Description: Periwinkle is a trailing plant about 6 inches high with small, oval, opposite, dark green, shiny, evergreen leaves. In spring, 5-petaled flowers, about ¾-inch in diameter, are borne on short stems in a lovely shade of blue.

Ease of care: Easy.

How to grow: Periwinkles will grow in full sun, but they prefer light or partial shade. Good, well-drained garden soil is best.

Propagation: By division or by cuttings.

Uses: An excellent ground cover, periwinkle is also a welcome change when planted along the edge of beds or borders and lining flagstone or brick walks.

Related varieties: 'Alba' has pure white flowers, larger than the species. 'Bowles' Variety' is more compact than the species, with profuse flowering into May.

Garden Phlox

Phlox paniculata
Zone: USDA 5

Phlox are very popular plants since they are easy to grow, great for color, and marvelous for cutting. By far the most popular are the garden phlox and, over the years, a number of lovely kinds have been developed. The genus is named for the Greek word for "flame" and refers to some of the brightly colored flowers.

Description: Clump-forming perennials with very strong stems, phlox bear simple, lance-shaped leaves. These are topped with clusters of usually fragrant, showy, 5-petaled flowers arising from a narrow tube. They bloom over a long period.

Ease of care: Easy.

How to grow: Garden phlox need good, well-drained soil in full sun or light shade, and plenty of water during the summer. Plants are often prone to powdery mildew. Keep individual plants 18 inches apart to promote air circulation. Divide plants every three years to keep them vigorous, and deadhead to prolong bloom.

Propagation: By division or by seed.

Uses: Phlox can be bunched by color or mixed, the taller types best at the rear of the border.

Related species: *Phlox carolina* (once called *P. suffruticosa*) are native American flowers from North Carolina west to Missouri and then south, hardy to USDA Zone 5. They bloom from June into July. Soil should be good and well-drained in full sun. 'Miss Lingard' bears clear white flowers on 30-inch stems, while 'Rosalinde' has clear pink flowers on 36-inch stems, often blooming from late June into

Pincushion Flower

Scabiosa caucasica
Zone: USDA 4

Pink, Carnation

Dianthus species
Zone: USDA 5

September. *Phlox divaricata,* or the wild sweet William, is another American native and a low-growing species, flowering in May and June, preferring partial shade. Hardy to USDA Zone 4, plants usually bloom at a height of 14 inches. 'Fuller's White' has pure white flowers. *Phlox stolonifera,* or creeping phlox, is another native wildflower, which crawls along the ground and bears purple or violet flowers on 6-inch stems in late spring. Plants are hardy to USDA Zone 4 and prefer light shade, but will take a half day of sun. 'Blue Ridge' has sky-blue flowers and 'Osborne's White' is pure white. *Phlox subulata,* or the mountain pink, is a creeping phlox used as a ground cover or in rock gardens, blooming in early spring. It is hardy in USDA Zone 4. Soil should be well-drained with full sun. Height is 6 inches.

Related varieties: 'Dodo Hanbury Forbes' is clear pink on 3-foot stems; 'The King' has deep purple flowers; 'Starfire' is a brilliant red; and 'White Admiral' is a pure white. All are on 30-inch stems. The Symons-Jeune strain of phlox was developed both for strength of stems and resistance to fungus—a problem that most of the phlox are susceptible to. Notable varieties are 'Blue Lagoon,' with large heads of lavender-blue flowers on 40-inch stems; 'Dresden China,' flowers of a soft shell-pink on 4-foot stems; and 'Gaiety,' with salmon blossoms with a cherry-red eye on 42-inch stems.

The pincushion flower was introduced to England in 1591 and has been a popular garden flower ever since. The common name refers to the flower heads that when closed resemble pincushions full of pins. The genus is named for "scabies," an itch that some species were said to cure.

Description: Plants have simple, lance-shaped, deeply cut leaves, with long, graceful flower stems growing to 2 feet high. They bear domed flower heads up to 3 inches across.

Ease of care: Easy.

How to grow: Scabiosas want good, well-drained garden soil in full sun. In areas of hot summers, light shade is welcomed. Remove dead flowers for a long period of bloom.

Propagation: By division in spring or by seed.

Uses: Plant scabiosas in drifts and along the edge of the bed or border. They are excellent as cut flowers.

Related varieties: 'Alba' has pure white flowers; 'Fama' has flowers of a true lavender; 'House's Hybrids' produce flowers about 2 inches in diameter in colors of blue, lavender, and white; and 'Miss Willmott' bears flowers in ivory white.

Pinks are the hardy flowers of the garden, and carnations are usually thought of as being the flower of the buttonhole or the bouquet, although the terms are often mixed. Regardless of the name, these flowers are known for both their blossoms and for the marvelous sweet and spicy scent that many produce. The genus is a Greek word for "divine flower."

Description: Plants have narrow leaves on jointed stems that end with 5-petaled flowers with fringed edges, often having a distinct odor.

Ease of care: Easy.

How to grow: Plants want full sun and a good, well-drained garden soil. Except for some of the alpine species, these plants are short-lived perennials and benefit from division every two or three years.

Propagation: By division, by cuttings, or by seed.

Uses: Pinks are excellent choices for a rock garden, hanging over the edges of a wall, or for the front of a garden, especially as edging plants. They make wonderful cut flowers, and many will bloom all summer if spent flowers are removed.

Related species: *Dianthus barbatus,* or Sweet William, produces clusters of varicolored flowers that are lovely in the border. They are usually thought of as biennials, but with self-seeding produce flowering plants year after year. *Dianthus deltoides,* or the maiden pink, forms low mats of leaves usually covered with

(continued)

129

Pink (continued)

Poppy

Papaver orientale
Zone: USDA 5

Plume Poppy

Macleaya cordata
Zone: USDA 4

delightful single flowers on 6- to 12-inch stems perfect for the rock garden. It needs good drainage. 'Brilliant' bears bright, double crimson flowers. *Dianthus gratianopolitanus,* or the cheddar pink, produces clouds of flowers on 6- to 8-inch stems perfect for the rock garden. The flowers are about 1 inch wide and beloved by butterflies. They are hardy in USDA 4. *Dianthus Knappii* comes from Yugoslavia and, unlike the other pinks in the clan, bears yellow flowers on 18-inch plants.

Related varieties: *Dianthus* x *Allwoodii* are hybrids produced years ago in England. The foliage is bluish-green, with flowers of red, pink, or white, often with darker centers, reaching a height of 18 inches. They must be divided every few years to survive. There are many cultivars available. 'Alpinus' is a dwarf growing up to 12 inches high; 'Blanche' is a glorious double white; and 'Robin' has bright red, double flowers.

Papaver is the ancient Latin name for the flowers and is thought to refer to the sound made in chewing the seeds.

Description: Basal leaves are covered with hairs. Graceful stalks grow to 4 feet and bear single or double flowers with petals of crepe paper texture surrounding many stamens. They flower in late May and June. Seedpods are attractive. Any part of the plant will bleed a milky sap when cut.

Ease of care: Easy.

How to grow: Poppies are very undemanding, wanting only good, well-drained soil in full sun. Drainage is especially important in the winter, as water will rot the roots. Place the crown 3 inches below the soil surface and mulch the first winter to prevent heaving. During heavy spring rains, try to cover the plant with Reemay cloth, a commercially available material that is very light and offers some protection. Plants go dormant in late summer, so their spaces should be filled with annuals or summer bulbs.

Propagation: By division in the fall or by seed.

Uses: Use poppies in beds or borders in combination with other perennials or in single groupings.

Related species: *Meconopsis cambrica,* or the Welsh poppy, has 4-petaled, orange or yellow flowers that close at night; adapt to light shade; and seed about the garden.

Related varieties: 'Carmen' bears brilliant red flowers; 'Harvest Moon' has flowers of orange-yellow; 'Lavender Glory' has deep lavender flowers with large, black basal spots; 'Maiden's Blush' has ruffled petals of white with a blush-pink edge; and 'White King' is white.

The plume poppy is a plant that every border should have. Even when not in bloom, it is lovely. Older books call it *Bocconia*. The genus is named in honor of Alexander Macleay, a Colonial Secretary for New South Wales.

Description: Large, lobed leaves, gray-green on top and white and downy underneath, are often 8 inches across on stems to 8 feet tall. Small, white flowers have up to 30 stamens that wave in the wind and bloom in late summer.

Ease of care: Easy.

How to grow: Plume poppies do well in average garden soil in full sun and partial shade in areas with very warm summers. If soil is fertile and dug deeply, plants will quickly spread. The stems are very strong and plants do not need staking.

Propagation: By division or by cuttings.

Uses: Unlike many plants in their height range, plume poppies look great from the ground up and should not be set behind other plants. They are great as specimen plants and also do well in pots.

Related species: *Macleaya microcarpa* 'Coral Plume' has coral-pink flowers with 8 to 12 stamens.

Japanese Primrose

Primula Sieboldii
Zone: USDA 5

In the garden world, there are over 400 species of primroses. Most primroses revel in an English climate calling for cool temperatures and plenty of rainfall and are at a loss in the often short spring and variable summers found over much of the United States. The species listed below performs well in this country. The genus name is a diminutive of the Latin *primus*, "first," alluding to the early flowering of certain European species.

Description: The basal foliage is a rosette with dark green, heart-shaped leaves with a scalloped edge. The plant bears tight bunches of 2-inch wide, pink or purple deckle-edged flowers on 12-inch stems. Each has a white "eye."

Ease of care: Easy.

How to grow: Japanese primroses require partial shade and a good, moist soil. Unlike other primroses, the leaves disappear and plants become dormant in the summer and are spared the rigors of drought and heat.

Propagation: By division or by seed.

Uses: Primroses are unexcelled for the woodland garden or for planting among spring wildflowers in a shady spot of the garden—even without bloom the foliage is very attractive. They make excellent cut flowers. Dormant plants may be potted up in late winter and forced into bloom at normal room temperatures.

Related varieties: The Barnhaven hybrids come in colors of frost-white, rose-red, lilac, China blue, and pink. Blossom shape varies from perfectly round to fringed to a snowflake form.

Rockcress

Aubrieta deltoidea
Zone: USDA 5

Rockcresses are trailing perennials that usually burst into glorious bloom in late April and May. Plants originally came from Greece and Sicily. The genus is named in honor of Claude Aubriet, a French botanical artist of the 1700s.

Description: Rockcresses are creeping and trailing plants with small and simple leaves covered with tiny hairs. They bear a wealth of 4-petaled flowers, each about ¾-inch wide and typically in blues, lilacs, and purples. Plant height is between 4 and 6 inches. The leaves are evergreen when given snow cover, but turn brown without.

Ease of care: Easy.

How to grow: Rockcresses prefer good soil with perfect drainage and a location in full sun. They will also do well in some shade and a very lean soil mix with a great deal of sand. After blooming is finished, they can be cut back.

Propagation: By division, by seed, or by cuttings.

Uses: Rockcresses are great for rock gardens, where they form large carpets of bloom. They can also be planted in pockets of stone walls and do well in trough gardens. In addition, they are fine for the edging of borders.

Related varieties: 'Purple Gem' bears purple flowers on 6-inch stems; 'Bengel' produces larger-than-average flowers in rose, lilac, and deep red; 'Dr. Mules' is an old garden favorite with violet-purple flowers. 'Novalis Blue Hybrid' is a new cultivar with a mid-blue color that comes from seed.

Rock Cress

Arabis caucasica
Zone: USDA 4

The rock cresses are charming plants that hug rock surfaces like rugs. The genus means "Arabia" and could refer to the fact that the plants revel in warm sand and sun.

Description: These creepers are made up of tufted rosettes of oval leaves covered with white down. In spring, they send up 1-foot stems covered with dozens of 4-petaled flowers, ½ inch wide and with a sweet scent.

Ease of care: Easy.

How to grow: The plants resent hot and damp summers and must have perfect drainage. Spent blossoms should be cut to neaten up the plants.

Propagation: By division in early spring or fall or by seed.

Uses: Rock cresses are best suited for a rock garden or for cultivation in a wall garden.

Related species: *Arabis Ferdinandi-Coburgi* 'Variegata' bears its white flowers on 5-inch stems and has creamy white and green leaves with a faint touch of pink. 'Flore-Pleno' is the double, white-flowered form with 10-inch stems; 'Snow Cap' is a single form with flowers on 8-inch stems; and 'Compinkie' bears rose-red flowers on 6-inch stems.

Rodgersia

Rodgersia aesculifolia
Zone: USDA 5

These are extremely handsome plants primarily grown for their foliage. The plants are named in honor of a United States admiral, John Rodgers, who commanded an expedition to Japan at the end of the 19th century, where one species (*Rodgersia podophylla*) was discovered.

Description: Rodgersia has large, compound leaves that resemble those of a horse chestnut. Each leaflet is about 7 inches long, coarsely toothed, and grows on 4-foot high plants that are usually tinted with bronze. Small, 5-petaled white flowers appear in July, blooming in flat clusters on 2-foot stems.

Ease of care: Moderately easy.

How to grow: Rodgersias need specific conditions that include a good, moist soil with plenty of organic matter mixed in and a location with the crowns at least 1 inch below the surface. They want partial shade with sun only part of the day, preferably in the morning. In areas of severe winter without snow cover, mulch is necessary.

Propagation: By division in spring or by seed.

Uses: Like ferns, rodgersias are special plants perfectly suited for the wild garden, the edge of the water garden, or the shade garden. They do especially well in open shade under tall trees.

Related species: *Rodgersia pinnata,* the feathered bronze leaf, has large, toothed, emerald-green, fanlike leaves tinged with bronze. Flowers are pink, and plants grow to about 36 inches high.

Christmas Rose, Lenten Rose, Hellebore

Helleborus species
Zone: USDA 4 to 5

Myth has it that an angel gave a Christmas rose to a young shepherdess who had no present for the infant Jesus. The genus is an ancient Greek name for the plant. The entire plant is deadly poisonous.

Description: Deeply divided, usually evergreen leaves grow from a thick rootstock, producing flowers with thick petals (really sepals) appearing in late fall, winter, or very early spring.

Ease of care: Easy.

How to grow: Hellebores require a good, deep, well-drained soil with plenty of humus and partial shade. When temperatures fall below 15° F, blooming is usually put off until the weather warms. At low temperatures, some protection is needed.

Propagation: By division or by seed.

Uses: The foliage alone is worth growing and makes an excellent ground cover. Flowers are good for cutting, and the plants can be grown in pots or in a greenhouse.

Related species: *Helleborus niger,* or the true Christmas rose, bears white or pinkish-green flowers, and blooms in late fall, winter, or early spring depending on the climate. Although hardy in USDA Zone 4, winters often make growing difficult. *Helleborus orientalis,* or the Lenten rose, is the easiest of the species to grow, with cream-colored flowers fading to brown amidst palmlike foliage. This variety is hardy in USDA Zone 5.

Related variety: 'Atrorubens' blooms in late winter or early spring, with deep maroon flowers.

Rock Rose, Sun Rose, Frostweed

Helianthemum nummularium
Zone: USDA 6

Even if the individual flowers of the rock rose last only one day, there are always more to come. The genus name is from the Greek for "sunflower."

Description: Sprawling and trailing evergreen shrubs with 2-inch leaves that are gray and woolly underneath bear lovely 5-petaled flowers that bloom from late spring into July.

Ease of care: Easy.

How to grow: Rock roses are undemanding plants, wanting only full sun and good, well-drained soil. They should be given winter protection in colder parts of Zone 6. If soil is too acid, add a cup of ground limestone per square yard into the soil surrounding the plant. If cut back after the first blooming, they should bloom again in late summer.

Propagation: By cuttings or by seed.

Uses: Since these plants are real sun-lovers, they are best in rock gardens, along flagstone paths, tumbling over the edge of a low wall, or set in the crevices between and alongside garden steps.

Related species: *Helianthemum apenninum* 'Roseum' has pink flowers on 10-inch stems.

Related varieties: 'Buttercup' bears golden-yellow flowers on 10-inch stems; 'Fire Dragon' has large, copper-red flowers in stark contrast to the gray-green foliage; and 'St. Mary's' blooms with pure white flowers.

Meadow Rue

Thalictrum aquilegifolium
Zone: USDA 5b

Meadow rues are tall and lovely plants with flowers that lack petals but have dozens of fluffy stamens. The English word "rue" refers to the resemblance between the leaves of these plants and the herb rue (*Ruta*). *Thalictrum* is an old Greek name for this genus.

Description: The leaves are compound (the species name means "leaves like an *Aquilegia* or columbine") on stout-branched stalks growing up to 4 feet tall. Plants bear clusters of rosy purple, petal-less flowers with many stamens, resembling balls of fluff. They bloom in late May and June.

Ease of care: Moderately easy.

How to grow: Soil for meadow rues should be moist with plenty of additional organic matter in partial shade. In cool gardens in the North, they can take full sun. In hot summers, they must have additional moisture.

Propagation: By division in early spring or by seed.

Uses: Use these plants in the wild garden where they naturalize with ease. They are also excellent at the back of a bed or border. Both flowers and foliage are good for bouquets.

Related species: *Thalictrum polygamum,* or tall meadow rue, is an American native wildflower often reaching a height of 10 feet when conditions are to its liking. The flowers are white. It works well in the back of the garden or in a swampy area of the wild or water garden. *Thalictrum speciosissimum* blooms in June with bright yellow flowers on 6-foot stalks and very attractive blue-green foliage.

Related variety: 'Album' has white flowers.

Russian Sage

Perovskia species
Zone: USDA 5

A plant of great charm, originally from Afghanistan and West Pakistan, Russian sage is aromatic in addition to being beautiful. The genus is named in honor of a provincial Russian governor, V. A. Perovski.

Description: A subshrub with a woody base produces gray-white stems up to 4 feet tall, bearing small, oval, aromatic leaves with gray-white hairs on the undersides. Sprays of small ¼-inch, violet-blue flowers appear in late July and August.

Ease of care: Easy.

How to grow: Well-drained soil and a spot in full sun are the requirements for these plants. They are not at all fussy. Cut any branches that remain after winter to the ground in early spring.

Propagation: By cuttings.

Uses: As a specimen, as a hedge, or planted in a mass, these late-flowering plants will always elicit comments from garden visitors. The flowers are excellent when cut.

Salvia, Meadow Sage

Salvia x *superba*
Zone: USDA 4

When people think of salvia they think of 'Blaze of Fire,' the variety of *Salvia splendens* from Brazil with its blatant scarlet blossoms, found in almost every public planting in America. But there are other perennial salvias with better colors and greater charm available for gardens. The genus name is the ancient Latin word *salveo,* "to heal," from the alleged medicinal qualities of some species.

Description: Salvia is a sterile hybrid found only in cultivation. It has gray-green, paired leaves covered with tiny hairs underneath on square stems growing up to 3 feet high. They bear spikes, or bracts, of violet-purple flowers that contain smaller true flowers.

Ease of care: Easy.

How to grow: Salvia are not fussy except that they need full sun and a good garden soil with excellent drainage.

Propagation: By division or by cuttings.

Uses: Use salvias in drifts—the effect will be one of many flower spikes.

Related species: *Salvia azurea,* or the blue salvia, is a native American plant reaching 5 feet in height and bearing deep blue flowers. 'Grandiflora' is a variety of the species. It has larger flowers.

Related varieties: 'Blue Queen' has deep violet flowers through June. 'East Friesland' (or 'Oestfroesland') has 18-inch spikes of violet-blue flowers of particular beauty. 'May Night' (or 'Mainacht') bears indigo flowers with purple bracts on 18-inch stems. Spent flowers should be cut back for rebloom.

Self-heal

Prunella Webbiana
Zone: USDA 5

The self-heals include a very common wildflower from Europe and Asia, *Prunella vulgaris*, believed to be a remedy for curing wounds and other ailments. The genus is named after *brunella* or *braune*, the German word for "quinsy," a disease of the throat the plants were thought to cure.

Description: Self-heals have simple leaves with prominent veins on the underside and square stems. Small flowers resembling snapdragons bloom in the summer in round spikes.

Ease of care: Easy.

How to grow: Self-heals prefer a good garden soil. In the cooler North full sun is fine, but in warmer areas of the country, partial shade and a moist soil are best.

Propagation: By division in spring or by seed.

Uses: Self-heals are a good ground cover in the wild garden and in shady areas along walkways, under taller plants, and in the rock garden.

Related varieties: 'Loveliness' has lilac flowers on 9-inch stems; 'Pink Loveliness' bears pink blossoms on 1-foot stems; 'Purple Loveliness' is a rich purple and has a vigorous habit that makes it a good ground cover; and 'White Loveliness' has pure white flowers on 8-inch stems.

Sneezeweed, Swamp Sunflower

Helenium autumnale
Zone: USDA 4

There are many plants that begin blooming in early fall in bright colors that can often match those of autumn leaves. Sneezeweed is one such flower. The genus name is from an ancient Greek word for a plant named after Helen of Troy. The common name refers to a profusion of golden pollen that could cause problems for allergy sufferers. They are native American plants.

Description: Small daisies have downturned ray flowers on stout stems that branch toward the top and can reach 6 feet. Basal rosettes of leaves are evergreen in areas of mild winters. Plants bloom from late August through September.

Ease of care: Easy.

How to grow: Although the plants are often found in dampish spots in the wild, swamp sunflowers can easily adapt to ordinary garden soil, especially in a low spot. During periods of drought, they need extra water. Nipping off the growing tips in the spring will help produce bushier plants.

Propagation: By division in spring or by seed.

Uses: Sneezeweed provides beautiful color for the back of a border or for an autumn or wild garden. They should be planted with ornamental grasses and with fall asters. They are excellent for cutting.

Related varieties: 'Riverton Beauty' has yellow flowers with a maroon eye; 'Butterpat' has flowers of clear yellow; and 'Moerheim Beauty' is bronze-red. All are on 4-foot stems.

Soapweed

Yucca glauca
Zone: USDA 5

These evergreen plants with swordlike leaves are hardy where the ground freezes and snow falls. The flower buds are edible and the fruits and roots can be substituted for soap. The genus is named for an entirely different Haitian plant.

Description: Short, prostrate stems form clumps of leaves, ½-inch wide and up to 36 inches long with narrow, white margins. Stems growing to 8 feet bear bell-shaped, greenish-white flowers 2 inches long, which turn up at night and become fragrant to lure moths for pollination. Fruits are pods.

Ease of care: Easy.

How to grow: Yuccas are adaptable to most situations, preferring full sun and good, well-drained garden soil. They have tap roots, so once planted they are best left alone.

Propagation: Seeds or occasional offsets on mature plants.

Uses: Since they have tap roots, yuccas are very drought-resistant and, once ensconced, can be left alone. They are excellent as specimen plants. Since they are evergreen, they should also be considered for the winter garden. The flowers are spectacular.

Related species: *Yucca filamentosa,* or Adam's needle, has 2½-foot leaves, their margins bearing threads. Flowers are creamy white and bell-shaped, on stalks often up to 12 feet high, but usually growing to about 6 feet. 'Gold Sword' has evergreen leaves with soft green margins and bright yellow centers.

Soapwort, Bouncing Bet

Saponaria officinalis
Zone: USDA 5

A European immigrant that has now natural-ized over much of North America, soapwort was brought over by the colonists to be used as a soap substitute. When bruised or boiled in water, the leaves produce a lather with detergent properties that even removes grease. The genus name refers to the Latin word *sapo,* meaning "soap."

Description: Soapwort has stout, 24-inch stems, swollen at the joints, with oval and opposite leaves. It bears pink or white 1-inch flowers in clusters, each with 5 united petals that are especially fragrant at night.

Ease of care: Easy.

How to grow: Saponarias want a good, well-drained soil in full sun, but they will also do well in a moist spot.

Propagation: By division or by seed.

Uses: Saponarias are useful in the wild garden, in the bed or border, and even to carpet a slope or bank.

Related species: *Saponaria Ocymoides,* or the rock soapwort, is a branching, trailing plant for the edge of the border or a rock wall, needing full sun and good drainage. Plants are usually 6 inches tall and covered in June with 5-petaled rose-pink flowers. 'Alba' has white flowers, and 'Splendens' bears deep rose-pink blossoms on 4-inch plants.

Related variety: 'Rubra Plena' is a form with double pink flowers.

Speedwell

Veronica spicata
Zone: USDA 5

Speedwell is a plant of the roadside with pretty flowers that "speed you well." In Ireland, a bit of the plant was pinned on to clothes to keep the traveler from accident. The flowers were named for St. Veronica.

Description: Plants have simple, oblong, 2-inch leaves usually opposite on strong stems. They grow to 18 inches, often bending, bearing densely branching spikes of small, blue or pink, 5-inch long flowers that bloom in summer.

Ease of care: Easy.

How to grow: Speedwells will succeed in any good, well-drained garden soil in full sun or partial shade. Be sure to deadhead for repeat bloom. Plants will not usually survive wet feet in winter.

Propagation: By division or by seed.

Uses: The taller varieties are beautiful in both bed and border as well as in the rock garden. They are good cut flowers.

Related species: *Veronica latifolia* is usually available only as 'Crater Lake Blue,' bearing flowers of a deep gentian-blue on 18-inch stems. *Veronica prostrata* is a mat-forming type with deep blue flowers on 4-inch stems. 'Heavenly Blue' is usually offered.

Related varieties: 'Blue Peter' bears deep blue flowers in July and August on 24-inch stems; 'Icicle' is pure white on 18-inch plants; 'Minuet' has silvery green leaves and bears pink flowers on 1-foot stems in June; 'Nana' has blue flowers on 8-inch stems; 'Red Fox' blooms with deep rose-red flowers on 14-inch stems; and 'Sunny Border Blue' has violet-blue spikes that bloom from June until hard frost.

Spiderwort

Tradescantia x *Andersoniana*
Zone: USDA 5

Spiderworts can be compared to daylilies and dayflowers—each blossom lasts only one day. The common name refers to the many glistening hairs on the sepals and the buds. They resemble a spider's nest of webs, especially when covered with dew ("wort" is an old English word for plant).

Description: Spiderworts are weak-stemmed plants that grow up to 1 foot long. They produce a watery juice and have folded, strap-like leaves. The 3-petaled flowers, opening at dawn and fading by mid-afternoon, are surrounded by many buds.

Ease of care: Easy.

How to grow: Spiderworts want a good, well-drained garden soil in full sun or partial shade. In dry summers, they will need extra water. In too-rich soil, they grow quickly and tumble about. Even the newest types can become floppy by midsummer—so when flowering is through, cut the plants to the ground, and they will often flower again.

Propagation: By division in spring or by seed.

Uses: Although fine in the sunny border, the newer spiderworts are best in areas of open shade, especially under tall trees.

Related species: *Tradescantia virginiana* is the original species and is still found in many old country gardens. The flowers are usually 1 inch wide, violet-purple, and often very floppy.

Related varieties: 'Red Cloud' has deep rose-red flowers; 'Zwanenberg' has very large, blue flowers; 'Snow Cap' is pure white; and 'Valor' is a deep red-purple. All grow to a height of 20 inches.

Cushion Spurge

Euphorbia epithymoides
Zone: USDA 5

These flowers are in the same genus as the familiar Christmas poinsettia. In both plants, the flowers are very small and what we perceive to be petals are really colored leaves (called bracts), in various reds and white in poinsettias and bright yellow in the spurges. They are named in honor of a Greek physician called Euphorbius.

Description: Cushion spurges are plants with a milky sap (irritating to some people), with oblong, green leaves, growing in a clump 12 to 14 inches high and covered with yellow to chartreuse bracts in spring—the color itself looks as though it were applied with an artist's airbrush. The leaves turn red in the fall.

Ease of care: Easy.

How to grow: Spurges prefer a good, well-drained garden soil in full sun and partial shade in hot climates.

Propagation: By seed.

Uses: The yellow glow of this plant is startling in spring. Plants are best in front of a low wall or grouped on a low bank.

Related species: *Euphorbia Myrsinites,* or the donkeytail spurge, has bright yellow bracts in early spring and bluish-gray leaves on 10-inch stems that turn pink in the summer. Plants sprawl and are best when tumbling over a low stone wall.

Stonecrop

Sedum spectabile
Zone: USDA 4

There are perhaps 600 species of these succulent herbs—mostly in the North Temperate Zone. Many make excellent garden subjects, but they are usually not found in most nursery centers and are only available from the various rock garden societies. The genus name is from the ancient Latin term, *sedere,* "to sit," referring to their low-spreading habit or possibly from *sedare,* "to quiet," alluding to their supposed sedative properties.

Description: Sedums have strong stems with succulent, usually alternate leaves. Terminal clusters of small, star-shaped flowers have 5 petals.

Ease of care: Easy.

How to grow: Sedums need only a good, well-drained garden soil in full sun. They withstand drought and do amazingly well in very poor soils.

Propagation: By seed, by leaf cuttings, or by division.

Uses: The tall sedums, like *Sedum spectabile,* are excellent in the bed and border, especially effective when planted in masses. The shorter, sprawling types are best for the rock garden. Most make excellent cut flowers.

Related species: *Sedum Aizoon* reaches a height of between 12 and 18 inches with yellow to orange flowers in summer. *Sedum kamtschaticum* is only 4 inches high and has deep green, scalloped leaves. It bears orange-yellow flowers from July to September. *Sedum Sieboldii* is often called the "October Daphne." It's a trailing plant with lightly scalloped leaves and lovely pink flowers appearing in late fall. Bloom is often killed by frost. *Sedum spurium*

Sundrop, Evening Primrose

Oenothera species
Zone: USDA 5

is a creeping sedum, evergreen even in Zone 5, and makes an excellent ground cover. 'Bronze Carpet' has leaves that are tinted bronze and bears pink flowers, while 'Dragon's Blood' has dark red flowers.

Related varieties: Probably one of the top ten perennials in the garden world today is 'Autumn Joy.' It is also known as 'Herbstfreude' or 'Indian Chief.' Although best in full sun, plants will take light shade. They are always attractive: whether in tight buds of a light blue-green atop 2-foot stems; rosy pink in early bloom; in late bloom as the flowers turn mahogany; or a russet-brown during the winter. *S. spectabile* 'Brilliant' opens its flowers a month ahead of 'Autumn Joy'; 'Meteor' bears carmine-red blossoms on 18-inch stems; and 'Variegatum' has carmine flowers and leaves variegated with areas of creamy white.

The day-bloomers in this genus are the sundrops, and the common name is a perfect choice for petals that look like molten gold. The night-bloomers are called the evening primrose. They are often found in old-time gardens. The genus is named for the Greek word *oinos,* "wine," and *thera,* "to hunt," because of confusion regarding this flower and another genus with roots possessing the aroma of wine.

Description: Simple alternate leaves on strong stems grow up to 2 feet high. They are topped by clusters of bright yellow, 4-petaled flowers up to 2 inches across that bloom in the summer. Basal rosettes are evergreen in colder areas.

Ease of care: Easy.

How to grow: Sundrops are extremely tolerant of poor soil and are very drought-resistant, but the ground must be well-drained and full sun is necessary. If given a spot in good soil, they become quite pushy, but are easily controlled since they are shallow-rooted.

Propagation: By division in spring or by seed.

Uses: Sundrops are perfect for the wild garden and can hold their own at the edge of a field or meadow. Most of the flowers can be gathered for winter bouquets because the seedpods are very attractive.

Related species: There are a number of species useful for the garden. *Oenothera fruticosa* is a wildflower of the eastern United States, with 2-inch yellow flowers on 1½- to 2-foot stems and is the type usually found in old gardens. 'Youngi' is offered by nurseries today. *Oenothera missourensis* stays about 1 foot high, but the blossoms are often showy and 4 inches wide. The trailing stems carry a succession of lemon-yellow flowers opening in early afternoon. They are especially suited for the rock garden where the stems can tumble about and because their soil must never stay wet for any length of time. The seedpods are very attractive. *Oenothera speciosa* is another wildflower that is a rampant spreader in the wild garden; 'Rosea,' with light pink flowers 2 inches in diameter on high stems, is excellent for border edging. *Oenothera tetragona* is often confused with *O. fruticosa.* Its chief claim to fame is the splendid 'Fireworks,' with brilliant yellow flowers on 18-inch stems.

Perennial Sunflower

Helianthus x *multiflorus*
Zone: USDA 5

Perennial sunflowers are very valuable for their late season bloom, as their bright yellow flowers combine well with goldenrods and fall asters in September. The genus is Greek for "sun flower."

Description: Perennial sunflowers are tall, robust plants with fibrous roots and large, rough, simple leaves on stout stems. Large, yellow, daisylike flowers bloom in September and October.

Ease of care: Easy.

How to grow: Sunflowers want full sun and good, moist garden soil with water provided during periods of drought. Some of the wild species can be invasive.

Propagation: By division or by seed.

Uses: Perennial sunflowers are best grown in the back of the border or in the wild garden.

Related species: *Helianthus angustifolius,* or the swamp sunflower, is native from New York to Florida and west to Texas where it grows in wet or boggy areas. If moved to good garden soil and provided with extra water during periods of drought, the 6-foot plants will bloom in September with 3-inch wide, yellow daisies. *Helianthus salicifolius,* or willow-leaved sunflowers, are American natives from the Midwest. Although the 2-inch wide sunflowers are pretty when blooming in the fall, this plant is used for its attractive foliage. Plants grow about 4 feet high and want only good, well-drained garden soil with a bit of lime added if necessary.

Related variety: 'Flore Pleno' is the typical cultivar with double blossoms that look more like chrysanthemums than sunflowers.

Globe Thistle

Echinops Ritro
Zone: USDA 4

Globe thistles are large and stalwart plants for beds and borders that produce attractive balls of small, individual flowers. The genus name is in honor of the hedgehog because of the plant's prickly aspect.

Description: Globe thistles are 1½-inch balls of metallic-blue blossoms on stout, ribbed stems and, depending on the variety, grow from 3 to 7 feet tall. The leaves have spiny edges and are white-woolly beneath. They bloom in July and August.

Ease of care: Easy.

How to grow: Globe thistles are not fussy as to soil and will do well in full sun or open shade. Once established, they are very drought-resistant. They seed about with ease.

Propagation: By division in the spring or by seed.

Uses: The larger species are impressive when used in background plantings or when grown as specimen plants. The smaller types are attractive in a bed or border or when spread throughout a wild garden. All look especially lovely when mixed with a planting of conifers.

Related species: *Echinops sphaerocephalus* is a species that is much taller, sometimes reaching 7 feet and best used where a strong statement is needed.

Related variety: 'Taplow Blue' has a more intense blue color in the flowers.

Thrift, Sea Pink

Armeria maritima
Zone: USDA 4

Thrifts are excellent for the rock or wall garden. The derivation of the genus name is supposedly Celtic, a fact not too surprising, as the plants are found naturally along the maritime shores of Europe, in addition to the Pacific Northwest and Newfoundland.

Description: Low, basal rosettes of grasslike, evergreen leaves form carpets. Plants bloom in the spring with tightly packed globes of pink flowers, often sending up a few pink flowers all summer long.

Ease of care: Easy.

How to grow: They are very easy to grow as long as the soil is well drained with a location in full sun. If the soil is too fertile or too moist, the plants will begin to rot in the center. Older plants frequently do.

Propagation: By division in early spring or by seed.

Uses: Thrifts can be used to carpet a sandy bank or a seaside garden and do well in terra-cotta pots in a cool greenhouse.

Related varieties: 'Vindictive' bears deep pink flowers on 6-inch stems; 'Launcheana' has flowers of deep rose; and 'Alba' exhibits white flowers.

Turtlehead, Balmony

Chelone glabra
Zone: USDA 4

The common name is well taken as these native American wildflowers do look like turtles with gaping mouths. Balmony is a corruption of "baldmoney," and the derivation is unknown. *Chelone* is the Latin name for a tortoise.

Description: Turtleheads have small, narrow clusters of white flowers, sometimes tinted pink, along 2- to 4-foot stalks. Leaves are glossy green and toothed.

Ease of care: Easy.

How to grow: Turtleheads need damp growing conditions in full sun or light shade. In the wild, plants are often found in that narrow line between the edge of a pond and the woods. The soil must be well laced with humus and peat moss when planting. When spring growth reaches about 6 inches, tips should be nipped to promote bushy plants. Turtleheads bloom from late summer into fall.

Propagation: By division in spring or by seed.

Uses: Turtlehead is a lovely flower for the bog or waterside garden. It should not be used in the border unless it can be watered when needed.

Related species: *Chelone Lyonii* is a pink-flowered species from the southern mountains that is hardy in the North, blooming a bit later in the season than *Chelone glabra*.

Red Valerian, Jupiter's-Beard

Centranthus ruber
Zone: USDA 5

Described in *The Englishman's Flora* as a "cheerful and blowzy plant," this flower first turned up in England in the 16th century. Once a member of the genus *Valeriana* (so named in honor of an obscure healer called Valerius), another common name is "bloody butcher." Plants are often sold as *V. coccineus*.

Description: Fragrant, ½-inch scarlet to red flowers grow in dense clusters on 2- to 3-foot stems, blooming over a long period.

Ease of care: Easy.

How to grow: Valerians are not fussy, needing only good, well-drained soil in full sun, although they will tolerate slight shade. Flowering stems should be cut down to promote new flowers.

Propagation: By division or by seed.

Uses: This plant is best when massed and is often naturalized on old walls and rock outcrops.

Related varieties: 'Roseus' bears rose-colored flowers; 'Alba' has white flowers; and 'Ruber Mixed' has rose, white, and maroon flowers.

Yellow Waxbell

Kirengeshoma palmata
Zone: USDA 6

Yellow waxbells are native to Japan and Korea and were brought to European gardens in 1892. After almost 100 years of garden exposure, it is rather odd that this lovely and elegant plant is still considered a rarity. The genus is Japanese for *ki*, "yellow," and *rengeshoma*, a native name for another autumn-blooming plant.

Description: The 8-inch long leaves resemble those of a maple tree but have black stems. Plants grow about 3 feet high and produce sprays of long-lasting, nodding, yellow blossoms with 5 waxy petals. It blooms in late summer and early autumn.

Ease of care: Easy.

How to grow: Yellow waxbells want partial shade and a good, deep, humus-rich, moist soil. They have the same needs as rhododendrons. Since growth begins in late spring, Northern areas can sometimes see frost damage by late frost.

Propagation: By division in spring or by seed.

Uses: Few plants are as effective in the bed or border as yellow waxbells, and they are best used as specimen plants.

Wormwood

Artemisia species
Zone: USDA 3

With the exception of *Artemisia lactiflora,* or mugwort, the rest of the wormwoods are best used for their foliage. The genus is named for the wife of Mausolus, an ancient king who built a giant tomb. Surprisingly, these plants are members of the daisy family and include sagebrush, common wormwood (the source of absinthe), and the herb tarragon.

Description: Wormwoods are shrublike plants usually with attractive silver-gray foliage and sprays of small, mostly unattractive flowers. The leaves and other plant parts are often aromatic.

Ease of care: Easy.

How to grow: Plants prefer poor and sandy soil over deep and fertile earth. They must have full sun and good drainage or the roots will soon rot. Do not bother with these plants in areas of high humidity and damp summers. In warmer gardens, they can become weedy.

Propagation: By division or by seed.

Uses: The larger plants can be used as backgrounds to perennial borders; individual plants can be set about the garden to act as foils to bright and colorful blossoms, especially those with white, pink, or lavender flowers. When dried, they are excellent in winter bouquets.

Related species: *Artemisia Abrotanum,* or southernwood, can be used as a deciduous hedge as it can grow to a height of 5 feet. *Artemisia Absinthium,* or common wormwood,

has shiny, silvery, cut foliage on 4-foot stems. 'Lambrook Silver' has leaves of a finer cut. *Artemisia lactiflora,* or white mugwort, is the only one of this group grown for the flowers, which are not really white but more of a cream color. Masses of these tiny blossoms crowd 5-foot stems, starting in late summer and on into autumn. This plant needs better soil than the others. Even though the stems are strong, they might need staking in areas with gusty summer storms. They make excellent cut flowers. *Artemisia ludoviciana,* or white sage, bears willowlike leaves of silvery grayish-white on 3-foot stems. The variety *albula* has a cultivar 'Silver King,' with beautiful foliage on 2-foot stems. *Artemisia Schmidtiana* 'Silver Mound' is a cultivar from Japan that grows in rounded balls with feathery, cut foliage about 20 inches wide. The mounds tend to spread with maturity and will eventually need to be divided. *Artemisia Stellerana,* or beach wormwood, is the only member to be somewhat inclined to humidity and is often found naturalized along sandy beaches of the Northeast. Plants grow about 2½ feet high with tiny, yellow flowers.

Yarrow

Achillea species
Zone: USDA 3b

Most people have seen the wild form of yarrow, *Achillea Millefolium,* a wildflower originally from Europe and western Asia. The botanical name refers to *Achilles,* the hero of Greek legend, who is said to have used a species to heal battlefield wounds.

Description: Yarrow will grow between 1 and 3 feet high, blooming from June until August, and often until frost. Flowers are small and arranged in flat heads on top of stout stems. The foliage is finely cut and resembles a fern. Most species are aromatic and smell of chamomile.

Ease of care: Easy.

How to grow: Yarrows are especially valuable as they are tolerant of drought and suitable for any reasonably fertile garden soil that has good drainage. Plants revel in full sun, although they will tolerate a small amount of shade. New plants should be spaced about 12 to 18 inches apart.

Propagation: By division in spring or fall.

Uses: Yarrow are especially suitable for the garden border and look well in masses. They are excellent both as cut flowers and dried for winter bouquets.

Related species: 'Coronation Gold' bears large heads of golden-yellow flowers and is excellent for drying. The wildflower *Achillea Millefolium* is suited for the meadow or wild garden; the cultivar *Achillea* 'Crimson Beauty' bears rose-red flowers on 2-foot stems; 'Moonshine' has sulfur-yellow flowers on 2-foot stems; *Achillea Ptarmica* 'The Pearl' blooms with small, round, white flowers like its namesake on 3- to 4-foot stems. This plant has unbroken, weedy leaves.

Index

COMMON NAME	BOTANICAL NAME	PAGE(S)
Ageratum, Hardy; Mist Flower	*Eupatorium coelestinum*	15, 21, 94
Anemone, Japanese	*Anemone* species	15, 16, 18, 19, 20, 21, 52, 94
Aster, Golden	*Chrysopsis mariana*	16, 19, 20, 21, 44, 45, 50, 51, 52, 53, 79, 94
Aster, Stoke's	*Stokesia laevis*	15, 16, 20, 95
Astilbe; Garden Spiraea	*Astilbe* species	15, 20, 88, 95
Avens	*Geum* species	15, 16, 20, 88, 96
Baby's Breath	*Gypsophila paniculata*	10, 15, 16, 20, 96
Balloon Flower	*Platycodon grandiflorus*	15, 20, 96
Basket-of-Gold; Goldentuft; Madwort	*Aurinia saxatilis*	16, 20, 45, 90, 97
Beard Tongue	*Penstemon barbatus*	15, 20, 21, 97
Bellflower	*Campanula* species	15, 16, 19, 20, 79, 90, 97–98
Bergamot; Bee-Balm; Oswego-Tea	*Monarda didyma*	15, 20, 88, 98
Bergenia, Heartleaf	*Bergenia cordifolia*	15, 20, 88, 98
Bishop's Hat; Barrenwort	*Epimedium* species	15, 90, 99

COMMON NAME	BOTANICAL NAME	PAGE(S)
Blanket Flower	*Gaillardia* x *grandiflora*	15, 16, 20, 99
Blazingstar; Gayfeather	*Liatris* species	15, 16, 20, 78, 99
Bleeding Heart	*Dicentra* species	10, 15, 16, 20, 21, 53, 79, 86, 88, 100
Bluestar; Blue-Dogbane; Blue-Star-of-Texas	*Amsonia tabernaemontana*	15, 20, 100
Boltonia	*Boltonia asteroides*	16, 21, 52, 100
Bowman's-Root	*Porteranthus trifoliata*	16, 101
Bugleweed	*Ajuga* species	15, 16, 36, 90, 101
Bugloss, Italian	*Anchusa azurea*	15, 20, 101
Bugloss, Siberian	*Brunnera macrophylla*	15, 102
Buttercup, Creeping	*Ranunculus repens*	16, 18, 20, 102
Butterfly Weed; Milkweed	*Asclepias tuberosa*	15, 16, 20, 50, 102
Candytuft	*Iberis sempervirens*	16, 20, 45, 79, 83, 90, 103
Cardinal Flower	*Lobelia Cardinalis*	15, 20, 88, 103
Chives, Chinese; Garlic Chives	*Allium tuberosum*	16, 21, 103
Chrysanthemum	*Chrysanthemum* species	10, 15, 19, 20, 21, 43, 44, 50, 51, 52, 80, 86, 104
Cinquefoil	*Potentilla thurberi*	20, 105
Clematis, Bush; Upright Clematis	*Clematis recta*	15, 16, 20, 21, 51, 105
Cohosh, Black	*Cimicifuga racemosa*	16, 20, 88, 105
Columbine	*Aquilegia* species	15, 20, 50, 53, 88, 90, 106
Coneflower, Purple	*Echinacea purpurea*	15, 16, 106
Coneflower, Yellow; Black-eyed Susan	*Rudbeckia fulgida*	16, 20, 51, 86, 107
Coralbell; Alumroot	*Heuchera sanguinea*	15, 20, 21, 53, 79, 90, 107
Coreopsis	*Coreopsis* species	16, 20, 21, 50, 53, 107
Crane's-Bill	*Geranium* species	15, 20, 108
Cupid's Dart	*Catananche caerulea*	15, 16, 20, 108
Daisy, Michaelmas	*Aster* species	15, 20, 21, 108–109
Daylily	*Hemerocallis* species	15, 19, 21, 51, 78, 86, 109
Delphinium; Larkspur	*Delphinium* species	10, 15, 21, 45, 46, 50, 52, 53, 79, 110
Edelweiss	*Leontopodium alpinum*	16, 20, 90, 110
Everlasting, Pearly	*Anaphalis* species	16, 21, 111
Fleabane	*Erigeron hybridus*	15, 20, 21, 111
Forget-Me-Not, Chinese	*Cynoglossum nervosum*	15, 20, 21, 111
Foxglove, Yellow	*Digitalis grandiflora*	4, 16, 21, 53, 79, 112
Gas Plant; Burning Bush	*Dictamnus albus*	15, 16, 20, 21, 73, 112
Gaura	*Gaura Lindheimeri*	16, 21, 112
Globeflower	*Trollius* x *cultorum*	16, 20, 88, 113
Goat's Beard; Wild Spirea	*Aruncus dioicus*	16, 20, 21, 88, 113
Goldenrod	*Solidago* hybrids	16, 21, 113
Goldenstar	*Chrysogonum virginianum*	16, 20, 88, 114
Goutweed; Ground Elder	*Aegopodium Podagraria*	16, 114
Grasses, Ornamental	*Gramineae* family	10, 114–115
Blue Oat Grass	*Helictrotrichon sempervirens*	16, 115
Feather Reed Grass	*Calamagrostis acutiflora stricta*	21, 115
Fountain Grass	*Pennisetum alopecuroides*	16, 21, 83, 115
Japanese Blood Grass	*Imperata cylindrica rubra*	16, 115
Maiden Grass	*Miscanthus sinensis* 'Gracillimus'	21, 83, 115
Sea Oats	*Chasmanthium latifolium*	16, 21, 115
Zebra Grass	*Miscanthus sinensis* 'Zebrinus'	16, 88, 115
Holly, Sea	*Eryngium* species	15, 21, 115
Hosta; Plantain Lily	*Hosta* species	5, 6, 10, 15, 16, 38, 51, 53, 83, 88, 116
Houttuynia	*Houttuynia cordata*	16, 117
Indigo, False; Wild Indigo	*Baptisia australis*	15, 19, 20, 117

COMMON NAME	BOTANICAL NAME	PAGE(S)
Inula	*Inula ensifolia*	16, 21, 118
Iris	*Iris* species	10, 15, 19, 20, 21, 32, 46, 50, 52, 53, 73, 75, 79, 88, 90, 92, 118–119
Knapweed	*Centaurea* species	15, 21, 119
Knotweed; Himalaya Fleece Flower	*Polygonum affine*	15, 20, 119
Ladybells	*Adenophora confusa*	21, 120
Lady's Mantle	*Alchemilla* species	16, 20, 90, 120
Lamb's-Ear; Lamb's-Tongue	*Stachys byzantina*	16, 90, 120
Lavender	*Lavandula angustifolia*	15, 21, 78, 83, 86, 121
Lavender, Sea	*Limonium latifolium*	15, 21, 121
Leopard's-bane	*Doronicum cordatum*	16, 20, 121
Ligularia	*Ligularia* species	16, 21, 88, 122
Lily, Blackberry; Leopard Lily	*Belamcanda chinensis*	16, 21, 122
Lily, Toad	*Tricyrtis hirta*	15, 21, 122
Lily Turf, Big Blue	*Liriope Muscari*	15, 16, 19, 21, 83, 86, 123
Loosestrife, Gooseneck	*Lysimachia clethroides*	16, 21, 123
Loosestrife, Purple	*Lythrum Salicaria*	15, 19, 21, 60, 86, 88, 123
Lungwort; Jerusalem Sage	*Pulmonaria officinalis*	15, 20, 124
Lupine	*Lupinus polyphyllus*	15, 21, 50, 52, 73, 124
Lupine, Carolina; Aaron's Rod	*Thermopsis caroliniana*	16, 20, 21, 124
Mallow	*Malva Alcea*	15, 16, 21, 50, 51, 125
Mallow, Rose; Swamp Mallow	*Hibiscus Moscheutos*	15, 21, 86, 125
Meadowsweet; Queen-of-the-Prairie	*Filipendula rubra*	15, 16, 19, 88, 125
Nettle, Dead	*Lamium maculatum*	15, 16, 20, 21, 126
Obedient Plant; False Dragonhead	*Physostegia virginiana*	15, 16, 21, 126
Ox-Eye; False Sunflower	*Heliopsis helianthoides*	16, 21, 126
Pachysandra; Japanese Spurge	*Pachysandra terminalis*	16, 127
Pea, Perennial; Sweet Pea	*Lathyrus latifolius*	15, 16, 21, 127
Peony	*Paeonia* species	10, 15, 20, 32, 43, 46, 52, 53, 73, 79, 127–128
Periwinkle; Myrtle	*Vinca minor*	15, 16, 20, 51, 128
Phlox, Garden	*Phlox paniculata*	15, 21, 45, 51, 52, 53, 79, 88, 128–129
Pincushion Flower	*Scabiosa caucasica*	15, 21, 50, 129
Pink; Carnation	*Dianthus* species	15, 19, 20, 43, 46, 50, 51, 53, 79, 90, 129–130
Poppy	*Papaver orientale*	15, 20, 32, 43, 51, 67, 73, 130
Poppy, Plume	*Macleaya cordata*	15, 16, 21, 90, 130
Primrose, Japanese	*Primula Sieboldii*	15, 20, 36, 51, 53, 88, 131
Rockcress	*Aubrieta deltoidea*	15, 20, 90, 131
Rock Cress	*Arabis caucasica*	15, 16, 20, 131
Rodgersia	*Rodgersia aesculifolia*	15, 16, 21, 88, 132
Rose, Christmas; Lenten Rose; Hellebore	*Helleborus* species	15, 16, 20, 132
Rose, Rock; Sun Rose; Frostweed	*Helianthemum nummularium*	15, 21, 90, 132
Rue, Meadow	*Thalictrum aquilegifolium*	15, 20, 133
Sage, Russian	*Perovskia* species	15, 21, 86, 133
Salvia; Meadow Sage	*Salvia* x *superba*	15, 21, 133
Self-heal	*Prunella Webbiana*	15, 21, 134
Sneezeweed; Swamp Sunflower	*Helenium autumnale*	16, 21, 134
Soapweed	*Yucca glauca*	16, 21, 135
Soapwort; Bouncing Bet	*Saponaria officinalis*	15, 16, 21, 90, 135
Speedwell	*Veronica spicata*	15, 21, 79, 135
Spiderwort	*Tradescantia* x *Andersoniana*	15, 21, 136
Spurge, Cushion	*Euphorbia epithymoides*	16, 136

COMMON NAME	BOTANICAL NAME	PAGE(S)
Stonecrop	*Sedum spectabile*	10, 15, 16, 19, 21, 53, 83, 86, 90, 136–137
Sundrop; Evening Primrose	*Oenothera* species	16, 20, 137
Sunflower, Perennial	*Helianthus* x *multiflorus*	16, 19, 21, 138
Thistle, Globe	*Echinops Ritro*	10, 15, 21, 79, 138
Thrift; Sea Pink	*Armeria maritima*	15, 20, 138
Turtlehead; Balmony	*Chelone glabra*	15, 16, 21, 139
Valerian, Red; Jupiter's-Beard	*Centhranthus ruber*	15, 21, 139
Waxbell, Yellow	*Kirengeshoma palmata*	16, 21, 139
Wormwood	*Artemisia* species	16, 19, 21, 140
Yarrow	*Achillea* species	15, 21, 50, 82, 140